The
Amateur Emigrant

From the Clyde to
Sandy Hook

BY

ROBERT LOUIS STEVENSON

With a Preface by
Mrs. Fanny Stevenson

CARROLL & GRAF PUBLISHERS, INC.
NEW YORK

This first Carroll & Graf edition, 1998, is a facsimile edition
of the first American printing of *The Amateur Emigrant*.

Carroll & Graf Publishers, Inc.
19 West 21st Street
New York, NY 10010-6805

Library of Congress Cataloging-in-Publication Data is available.

ISBN: 0-7867-0572-8

Manufactured in the United States of America

TO

ROBERT ALAN MOWBRAY STEVENSON.

Our friendship was not only founded before we were born by a community of blood, but is in itself near as old as my life. It began with our early ages, and, like a history, has been continued to the present time. Although we may not be old in the world, we are old to each other, having so long been intimates. We are now widely separated, a great sea and continent intervening; but memory, like care, mounts into iron ships and rides post behind the horseman. Neither time nor space nor enmity can conquer old affection; and as I dedicate these sketches, it is not to you only, but to all in the old country, that I send the greeting of my heart.

R. L. S.

1879.

PREFACE

O NE of the closest friends of my husband's youth was a clever young man whose life, up to that time, had been mostly spent in hospitals. Embittered by poverty and suffering, his turbulent spirit revolted against law and society, and he had become an ardent socialist. I remember meeting, in his house, a party of Russian anarchists, Stepniak among them, who greeted him as "brother," shouting and laughing like schoolboys on a holiday, and declaring that if they could only meet my husband face to face they would soon make a convert of him. Indeed, up to a certain point, he sympathized with the socialists. He could not think of the innocent victims of civilization—the men who only asked for work, and could get none, while their children were starving —without raging against the existing order of things; while his own comfortable circumstances filled him with shame when he contemplated the hardships of those less fortunate than himself. But, unlike his friend, he could suggest no remedy; the assassination of individuals and bomb-throwing seeming to him not only barbaric, but silly and futile.

While he could see no royal road for others, the path for himself showed plainly enough before him, and it was his duty to swerve neither to the right nor the left. He believed he had no rights, only undeserved indulgences.

He must not eat unearned bread, but must pay the world, in some fashion, for what it gave him,—first, materially, then in kindness, sympathy, and love. Class distinctions, so strictly observed in England, he could not tolerate and never gave the slightest heed to their limitations. "Ladies?" he said in reply to an observation by a visitor, "one of the truest ladies in Bournemouth, Mrs. Waats, is at this moment washing my study windows." Once, coming upon a crowd of young roughs who were tormenting a wretched drunken creature of the streets, he pushed his way through them, and amid their jeers offered his arm to the woman and escorted her to the place she called home. "Don Quixote," he once said to my son, with a startled look, "why, *I* am Don Quixote!" Too much ease frightened him; he would occasionally insist on some sharp discomfort, such as sleeping on a mat on the floor, or dining on a ship's biscuit, to awaken him, as he said, to realities; and nothing pleased him more than to risk his life or health to serve another. Yet he never succeeded in wholly subduing the "old Adam" within him. Meanness or falsity or cruelty set his eyes blazing, and his language on such occasions became far from parliamentary.

Naturally his first visit to America, a land without class distinctions, was to him an event of extraordinary interest. The privations he endured as an amateur emigrant caused him much less suffering than his friends, who could not imagine themselves in a similar position, supposed. It was not the first time he had associated with the working-man on terms of equality; nor did it occur to him that it was a condescension on his part to join with his fellow-passengers in their attempts to make the time pass

pleasantly, or to do for them what little kindly offices came
in his way. One thing he did resent with bitterness—the
visits of the first-class passengers, who came out of curiosity into the steerage, looking about as though they were
passing through a menagerie. He never forgave "your wife,
my good man?" "Why," he would ask, "should I be her
good man any more than she my good woman? Her
question, and manner of putting it, made me understand
a great many things."

I remember, when we were living in Hyères, his receiving a letter from England that enclosed a petition asking
for the release of a noted anarchist who was said to be
dying in a French prison. This man, said the letter, had
thrown everything away for the "cause,"—his entire
fortune, his title, and his birthright as a subject of Russia,
to which he could never return; while comparatively young
in years, he presented the appearance of an old man, with
hair prematurely white and his health broken by confine-
ment in a damp, unsanitary prison. My husband's name
was to head the list. "Poor devil," he said, as he dipped his
pen in the ink. But he laid it down again thoughtfully,
and, instead of signing the petition, wrote a letter stating
that he had read the trial, and asking why the Russian gentleman had refused to say whether he had had a hand in
the blowing up of a workingman's café in Lyons, in which
catastrophe many persons, mostly peasants with their families, had been killed or shockingly injured. He could not,
he said, withhold his admiration for a man who had given
so much, but he could and would withhold his signature
until he was satisfied on this point. No such assurance
being forthcoming, the petition was returned with the

remark "I think Monsieur—had better complete his sacrifice by dying in prison."

For street musicians and wandering performers—acrobats, jugglers, etc.—my husband showed an understanding and sympathy that always won their confidence. "We're in the same boat," he would say, "earning our bread by amusing the public." "I always divide with a brother artist," he would remark, as he emptied his pockets into their hands. His acquaintance with such people, and his knowledge of the lives they led, gave him an almost morbid sense of the pitiless cruelty of modern civilization. It was only his strong intelligence and common sense that kept him from the ranks of the anarchists. He came to America with exaggerated views of the meaning of democracy, believing that there he would find the ideal social as well as political life. In the beginning he encountered many rude shocks, but he soon readjusted his point of view, though he never ceased regretting that this great country should have been lost to England. The name of George the Third was hardly to be spoken in his presence. "Had it not been for that idiot," he would cry, "we should now be one nation." Of New York, at this time, he saw very little, but on a later visit grew to love it as he would not have thought possible when he first arrived in America. A particularly attractive spot to him was Washington Square, where he spent many hours sitting on the benches under the trees enjoying the frank conversation of the children who used the park as a playground. On one memorable occasion he passed an afternoon there with Mark Twain.

At first the apparent rudeness of the average American

repelled him, but when he found that the gentlest, most kindly acts accompanied the off-hand address, his heart warmed towards his "younger brother." In San Francisco he made many friendships that were only broken by death,—Mr. and Mrs. Virgil Williams, to whom he dedicated *The Silverado Squatters:* Dr. Chismore, Dr. Willy, Judge Rearden, who recognized a kindred spirit in the unknown, shabbily dressed young Scot living in the poor little lodging house on Bush Street kept by Mr. and Mrs. Carson. For the last few years on each thirteenth of November a small band of those who love to do honour to my husband's memory have met in San Francisco to celebrate his birthday. Nor would the party be considered complete without Jules Simoneau, now far past eighty years of age, but still as clear in mind and as strong in heart as when my husband first knew him in Monterey, the best beloved of all the friends of that time of adversity.

The journey by emigrant train across the continent was an experience far worse than that on shipboard, but through all the fatigue and active misery of it my husband managed to keep his diary posted up to date, and two months later, in Monterey, he wrote to Mr. Colvin: *"The Amateur Emigrant* is about half drafted. It was from Monterey that he also wrote to Mr. Colvin: "I am a reporter for the *Monterey Californian* at a salary of two dollars a week!" From this feeble joke the most foolish tales have arisen, and grown in the retelling, of his having been a reporter connected with a San Francisco paper. The *Monterey Californian* was a tiny sheet that was hardly in a position to pay any one so much as two dollars a week. The editor was also the printer and did all the work on his paper with his own hands. The idea of a reporter in a place where "the population is about that of a dissenting chapel on a wet Sunday...mostly Mexican and Indian," was thought very amusing by both my husband and Mr. Bronson, the editor, but some one seems to have taken it very seriously.

The Amateur Emigrant was partly written in Monterey, and almost finished in San Francisco under the most depressing circumstances of ill health, poverty, and letters of adverse criticism from friends in England. In an unfinished letter dated Calistoga, June 4, 1880, he writes: "Today at last I send the last of the Double Damned Emigrant. It was all written, after a fashion, months ago, before I caved in; yet I have not had the pluck and strength to finish copying these few sheets before to-day. The attempt has cost me many a heavy heart....I have done a quaint action—I have sent three of my poems to the *Atlantic Monthly*, and a fourth, heaven of heavens! to Stephen![1] I am not mad; only a poet."

F. V. DE G. S.

[1] Leslie Stephen, at that time editing an English magazine.

TABLE OF CONTENTS.

The Second Cabin

I FIRST encountered my fellow-passengers on the Broomielaw in Glasgow. Thence we descended the Clyde in no familiar spirit, but looking askance on each other as on possible enemies. A few Scandinavians, who had already grown acquainted on the North Sea, were friendly and voluble over their long pipes; but among English speakers distance and suspicion reigned supreme. The sun was soon overclouded, the wind freshened and grew sharp as we continued to descend the widening estuary; and with the falling temperature the gloom among the passengers increased. Two of the women wept. Any one who had come aboard might have supposed we were all absconding from the law. There was scarce a word interchanged, and no common sentiment but that of cold united us, until at length, having touched at Greenock, a pointing arm and a rush to the starboard now announced that our ocean steamer was in sight. There she lay in mid-river, at the tail of the Bank, her sea-signal flying : a wall of bulwark, a street of white deck-houses, an aspiring forest of spars, larger than a church, and soon to be as populous as many an incorporated town in the land to which she was to bear us.

I was not, in truth, a steerage passenger. Although anxious to see the worst of emigrant life, I had some work to finish on the voyage, and was advised to go by the second cabin, where at least I should have a table at command. The advice was excellent ; but to understand the choice, and what I gained, some outline of the internal disposition of the ship will first be necessary. In her very nose is Steerage No. 1, down two pair of stairs. A little abaft, another companion, labelled Steerage No. 2 and 3, gives admission to three galleries, two running forward towards Steerage No. 1, and the third aft towards the engines. The starboard forward gallery is the second cabin. Away abaft the engines and below the officers' cabins, to complete our survey of the vessel, there is yet a third nest of steerages, labelled 4 and 5. The second cabin, to return, is thus a modified oasis in the very heart of the steerages. Through the thin partition you can hear the steerage passengers being sick, the rattle of tin dishes as they sit at meals, the varied accents in which they converse, the crying of their children terrified by this new experience, or the clean flat smack of the parental hand in chastisement.

There are, however, many advantages

for the inhabitant of this strip. He
does not require to bring his own bedding or dishes, but finds berths and a
table completely if somewhat roughly
furnished. He enjoys a distinct superiority in diet; but this, strange to say,
differs not only on different ships, but
on the same ship according as her head
is to the east or west. In my own experience, the principal difference between
our table and that of the true steerage
passenger was the table itself, and
the crockery plates from which we ate.
But lest I should show myself ungrate-
ful, let me recapitulate every advantage.
At breakfast, we had a choice between
tea and coffee for beverage; a choice
not easy to make, the two were so surprisingly alike. I found that I could
sleep after the coffee and lay awake after
the tea, which is proof conclusive of
some chemical disparity; and even by
the palate I could distinguish a smack

of snuff in the former from a flavour of
boiling and dish-cloths in the second.
As a matter of fact, I have seen passengers, after many sips, still doubting
which had been supplied them. In the
way of eatables at the same meal we
were gloriously favoured; for in addition to porridge, which was common to
all, we had Irish stew, sometimes a bit
of fish, and sometimes rissoles. The
dinner of soup, roast fresh beef, boiled
salt junk, and potatoes, was, I believe,
exactly common to the steerage and the
second cabin; only I have heard it
rumoured that our potatoes were of a
superior brand; and twice a week, on
pudding days, instead of duff, we had a
saddle-bag filled with currants under the
name of a plum-pudding. At tea we
were served with some broken meat from
the saloon; sometimes in the comparatively elegant form of spare patties or
rissoles; but as a general thing, mere

chicken-bones and flakes of fish, neither hot nor cold. If these were not the scrapings of plates their looks belied them sorely; yet we were all too hungry to be proud, and fell to these leavings greedily. These, the bread, which was excellent, and the soup and porridge which were both good, formed my whole diet throughout the voyage; so that except for the broken meat and the convenience of a table I might as well have been in the steerage outright. Had they given me porridge again in the evening, I should have been perfectly contented with the fare. As it was, with a few biscuits and some whisky and water before turning in, I kept my body going and my spirits up to the mark.

The last particular in which the second cabin passenger remarkably stands ahead of his brother of the steerage is one altogether of sentiment. In the steerage there are males and females; in

the second cabin ladies and gentlemen.
For some time after I came aboard I
thought I was only a male; but in the
course of a voyage of discovery between
decks, I came on a brass plate, and
learned that I was still a gentleman.
Nobody knew it, of course. I was lost
in the crowd of males and females, and
rigorously confined to the same quarter
of the deck. Who could tell whether I
housed on the port or star-board side of
steerage No. 2 and 3 ? And it was only
there that my superiority became practical; everywhere else I was incognito,
moving among my inferiors with simplicity, not so much as a swagger to
indicate that I was a gentleman after
all, and had broken meat to tea. Still,
I was like one with a patent of nobility
in a drawer at home; and when I felt
out of spirits I could go down and
refresh myself with a look of that brass
plate.

For all these advantages I paid but
two guineas. Six guineas is the steerage fare ; eight that by the second cabin ;
and when you remember that the steerage passenger must supply bedding and
dishes, and, in five cases out of ten,
either brings some dainties with him, or
privately pays the steward for extra
rations, the difference in price becomes
almost nominal. Air comparatively fit
to breathe, food comparatively varied,
and the satisfaction of being still privately a gentleman, may thus be had
almost for the asking. Two of my fellow-passengers in the second cabin had
already made the passage by the cheaper
fare, and declared it was an experiment
not to be repeated. As I go on to tell
about my steerage friends, the reader
will perceive that they were not alone in
their opinion. Out of ten with whom I
was more or less intimate, I am sure not
fewer than five vowed, if they returned,

to travel second cabin ; and all who had left their wives behind them assured me they would go without the comfort of their presence until they could afford to bring them by saloon.

Our party in the second cabin was not perhaps the most interesting on board. Perhaps even in the saloon there was as much good-will and character. Yet it had some elements of curiosity. There was a mixed group of Swedes, Danes, and Norsemen, one of whom, generally known by the name of 'Johnny,' in spite of his own protests, greatly diverted us by his clever, cross-country efforts to speak English, and became on the strength of that an universal favourite—it takes so little in this world of shipboard to create a popularity. There was, besides, a Scots mason, known from his favourite dish as 'Irish Stew," three or four nondescript Scots, a fine young Irishman,

O'Reilly, and a pair of young men who deserve a special word of condemnation. One of them was Scots; the other claimed to be American; admitted, after some fencing, that he was born in England; and ultimately proved to be an Irishman born and nurtured but ashamed to own his country. He had a sister on board, whom he faithfully neglected throughout the voyage, though she was not only sick, but much his senior, and had nursed and cared for him in childhood. In appearance he was like an imbecile Henry the Third of France. The Scotsman, though perhaps as big an ass, was not so dead of heart; and I have only bracketed them together because they were fast friends, and disgraced themselves equally by their conduct at the table.

Next, to turn to topics more agreeable, we had a newly married couple, devoted to each other, with a pleasant story of how they had first seen each other years ago at a preparatory school, and that very afternoon he had carried her books home for her. I do not know if this story will be plain to Southern readers; but to me it recalls many a school idyll, with wrathful swains of eight and nine confronting each other stride-legs, flushed with jealousy; for to carry home a young lady's books was both a delicate attention and a privilege.

Then there was an old lady, or indeed I am not sure that she was as much old as antiquated and strangely out of place, who had left her husband, and was traveling all the way to Kansas by herself. We had to take her own word that she was married; for it was sorely contradicted by the testimony of her appearance. Nature seemed to have sanctified her for the single state; even the colour of her hair was incompatible

2

with matrimony, and her husband, I thought, should be a man of saintly spirit and phantasmal bodily presence. She was ill, poor thing ; her soul turned from the viands; the dirty tablecloth shocked her like an impropriety ; and the whole strength of her endeavour was bent upon keeping her watch true to Glasgow time till she should reach New York. They had heard reports, her husband and she, of some unwarrantable disparity of hours between these two cities; and with a spirit commendably scientific, had seized on this occasion to put them to the proof. It was a good thing for the old lady; for she passed much leisure time in studying the watch. Once, when prostrated by sickness, she let it run down. It was inscribed on her harmless mind in letters of adamant that the hands of a watch must never be turned backwards ; and so it behooved her to lie in wait for the exact moment ere she started it again. When she imagined this was about due, she sought out one of the young second-cabin Scotsmen, who was embarked on the same experiment as herself and had hitherto been less neglectful. She was in quest of two o'clock; and when she learned it was already seven on the shores of Clyde, she lifted up her voice and cried 'Gravy!' I had not heard this innocent expletive since I was a young child; and I suppose it must have been the same with the other Scotsmen present, for we all laughed our fill.

Last but not least, I come to my excellent friend Mr. Jones. It would be difficult to say whether I was his right-hand man, or he mine, during the voyage. Thus at table I carved, while he only scooped gravy; but at our concerts, of which more anon, he was the president who called up performers to sing,

and I but his messenger who ran his
errands and pleaded privately with the
over-modest.   I knew I liked Mr. Jones
from the moment I saw him.   I thought
him by his face to be Scottish; nor
could his accent undeceive me.   For as
there is a *lingua franca* of many
tongues on the moles and in the feluc-
cas of the Mediterranean, so there is a
free or common accent among English-
speaking men who follow the sea. They
catch a twang in a New England port;
from a cockney skipper, even a Scotsman sometimes learns to drop an *h;* a
word of a dialect is picked up from
another hand in the forecastle; until
often the result is undecipherable, and
you have to ask for the man's place of
birth.   So it was with Mr. Jones.   I
thought him a Scotsman who had been
long to sea; and yet he was from
Wales, and had been most of his life a
blacksmith at an inland forge; a few

years in America and half a score of
ocean voyages having sufficed to modify
his speech into the common pattern.
By his own account he was both strong
and skilful in his trade. A few years
back, he had been married and after a
fashion a rich man; now the wife was
dead and the money gone. But his was
the nature that looks forward, and goes
on from one year to another and
through all the extremities of fortune
undismayed; and if the sky were to fall
to-morrow, I should look to see Jones,
the day following, perched on a step-
ladder and getting things to rights.
He was always hovering round inven-
tions like a bee over a flower, and lived
in a dream of patents. He had with
him a patent medicine, for instance, the
composition of which he had bought
years ago for five dollars from an American peddler, and sold the other day
for a hundred pounds (I think it was)

to an English apothecary. It was
called Golden Oil, cured all maladies
without exception; and I am bound to
say that I partook of it myself with
good results. It is a character of the
man that he was not only perpetually
dosing himself with Golden Oil, but
wherever there was a head aching or a
finger cut, there would be Jones with his
bottle.

If he had one taste more strongly
than another, it was to study character.
Many an hour have we two walked upon
the deck dissecting our neighbors in a
spirit that was too purely scientific to be
called unkind; whenever a quaint or
human trait slipped out in conversation,
you might have seen Jones and me
exchanging glances; and we could
hardly go to bed in comfort till we had
exchanged notes and discussed the day's
experience. We were then like a couple
of anglers comparing a day's kill. But

the fish we angled for were of a meta-
physical species, and we angled as often
as not in one another's baskets. Once,
in the midst of a serious talk, each found
there was a scrutinising eye upon himself; I own I paused in embarrassment
at this double detection; but Jones, with
a better civility, broke into a peal of
unaffected laughter, and declared, what
was the truth, that there was a pair of
us indeed.

Early Impressions

WE steamed out of the Clyde on
Thursday night, and early on
the Friday forenoon we took in our last
batch of emigrants at Lough Foyle, in
Ireland, and said farewell to Europe.
The company was now complete, and
began to draw together, by inscrutable
magnetisms, upon the decks. There
were Scots and Irish in plenty, a few
English, a few Americans, a good hand-
ful of Scandinavians, a German or two,
and one Russian; all now belonging for
ten days to one small iron country on
the deep.

As I walked the deck and looked
round upon my fellow-passengers, thus
curiously assorted from all northern
Europe, I began for the first time to

understand the nature of emigration. Day by day throughout the passage, and thenceforward across all the States, and on to the shores of the Pacific, this knowledge grew more clear and melancholy. Emigration, from a word of the most cheerful import, came to sound most dismally in my ear. There is nothing more agreeable to picture and nothing more pathetic to behold. The abstract idea, as conceived at home, is hopeful and adventurous. A young man, you fancy, scorning restraints and helpers, issues forth into life, that great battle, to fight for his own hand. The most pleasant stories of ambition, of difficulties overcome, and of ultimate success, are but as episodes to this great epic of self-help. The epic is composed of individual heroisms; it stands to them as the victorious war which subdued an empire stands to the personal act of bravery which spiked a single cannon and was adequately rewarded with a medal. For in emigration the young men enter direct and by the shipload on their heritage of work; empty continents swarm, as at the bo'sun's whistle, with industrious hands, and whole new empires are domesticated to the service of man.

This is the closet picture, and is found, on trial, to consist mostly of embellishments. The more I saw of my fellow-passengers, the less I was tempted to the lyric note. Comparatively few of the men were below thirty; many were married, and encumbered with families; not a few were already up in years; and this itself was out of tune with my imaginations, for the ideal emigrant should certainly be young. Again, I thought he should offer to the eye some bold type of humanity, with bluff or hawk-like features, and the stamp of an eager and pushing disposition. Now

those around me were for the most part
quiet, orderly, obedient citizens, family
men broken by adversity, elderly youths
who had failed to place themselves in life,
and people who had seen better days.
Mildness was the prevailing character;
mild mirth and mild endurance.   In a
word I was not taking part in an impetu-
ous and conquering sally, such as swept
over Mexico or Siberia, but found
myself, like Marmion, 'in the lost battle, borne down by the flying.'

Labouring mankind had in the last
years, and throughout Great Britain,
sustained a prolonged and crushing
series of defeats.   I had heard vaguely
of these reverses; of whole streets of
houses standing deserted by the Tyne,
the cellar-doors broken and removed for
firewood; of homeless men loitering at
the street-corners of Glasgow with their
chests beside them ; of closed factories,
useless strikes, and starving girls.   But

I had never taken them home to me or represented these distresses livingly to my imagination. A turn of the market may be a calamity as disastrous as the French retreat from Moscow; but it hardly lends itself to lively treatment, and makes a trifling figure in the morning papers. We may struggle as we please, we are not born economists. The individual is more affecting than the mass. It is by the scenic accidents, and the appeal to the carnal eye, that for the most part we grasp the significance of tragedies. Thus it was only now, when I found myself involved in the rout, that I began to appreciate how sharp had been the battle. We were a company of the rejected; the drunken, the incompetent, the weak, the prodigal, all who had been unable to prevail against circumstances in the one land, were now fleeing pitifully to another; and though one or two might still succeed, all had already failed. We were a shipful of failures, the broken men of England. Yet it must not be supposed that these people exhibited depression. The scene, on the contrary, was cheerful. Not a tear was shed on board the vessel. All were full of hope for the future, and showed an inclination to innocent gaiety. Some were heard to sing, and all began to scrape acquaintance with small jests and ready laughter.

The children found each other out like dogs, and ran about the decks scraping acquaintance after their fashion also. 'What do you call your mither?' I heard one ask. 'Mawmaw,' was the reply, indicating, I fancy, a shade of difference in the social scale. When people pass each other on the high seas of life at so early an age, the contact is but slight, and the relation more like what we may imagine to be the friend-

ship of flies than that of men ; it is so
quickly joined, so easily dissolved, so
open in its communications and so
devoid of deeper human qualities. The
children, I observed, were all in a band,
and as thick as thieves at a fair, while
their elders were still ceremoniously
manœuvring on the outskirts of acquaintance. The sea, the ship, and the seamen were soon as familiar as home to
these half-conscious little ones. It was
odd to hear them, throughout the voyage, employ shore words to designate
portions of the vessel. ' Co ' 'way doon
to yon dyke,' I heard one say, probably
meaning the bulwark. I often had
my heart in my mouth, watching them
climb into the shrouds or on the rails,
while the ship went swinging through
the waves; and I admired and envied
the courage of their mothers, who sat
by in the sun and looked on with composure at these perilous feats. ' He 'll

maybe be a sailor,' I heard one
remark ; 'now 's the time to learn.' I
had been on the point of running forward to interfere, but stood back at that,
reproved. Very few in the more delicate classes have the nerve to look upon
the peril of one dear to them ; but the
life of poorer folk, where necessity is so
much more immediate and imperious,
braces even a mother to this extreme of
endurance. And perhaps, after all, it is
better that the lad should break his
neck than that you should break his
spirit.

And since I am here on the chapter
of the children, I must mention one little fellow, whose family belonged to
Steerage No. 4 and 5, and who, where-
ever he went, was like a strain of music
round the ship. He was an ugly, merry,
unbreeched child of three, his lint-white
hair in a tangle, his face smeared with
suet and treacle ; but he ran to and fro

with so natural a step, and fell and picked himself up again with such grace and good-humour, that he might fairly be called beautiful when he was in motion. To meet him, crowing with laughter and beating an accompaniment to his own mirth with a tin spoon upon a tin cup, was to meet a little triumph of the human species. Even when his mother and the rest of his family lay sick and prostrate around him, he sat upright in their midst and sang aloud in the pleasant heartlessness of infancy.

Throughout the Friday, intimacy among us men made but a few advances. We discussed the probable duration of the voyage, we exchanged pieces of information, naming our trades, what we hoped to find in the new world, or what we were fleeing from in the old ; and, above all, we condoled together over the food and the vileness of the steerage. One or two had been so near

3

famine that you may say they had run
into the ship with the devil at their
heels ; and to these all seemed for the
best in the best of possible steamers.
But the majority were hugely discon-
tented. Coming as they did from a
country in so low a state as Great
Britain, many of them from Glasgow,
which commercially speaking was as
good as dead, and many having long
been out of work, I was surprised to
find them so dainty in their notions.   I
myself lived almost exclusively on bread,
porridge, and soup, precisely as it was
supplied to them, and found it, if not
luxurious, at least sufficient.   But these
working men were loud in their outcries.   It was not 'food for human
beings,' it was 'only fit for pigs,' it was
'a disgrace.'   Many of them lived
almost entirely upon biscuit, others on
their own private supplies, and some
paid extra for better rations from the

ship. This marvellously changed my notion of the degree of luxury habitual to the artisan. I was prepared to hear him grumble, for grumbling is the traveller's pastime; but I was not prepared to find him turn away from a diet which was palatable to myself. Words I should have disregarded, or taken with a liberal allowance; but when a man prefers dry biscuit there can be no question of the sincerity of his disgust.

With one of their complaints I could most heartily sympathise. A single night of the steerage had filled them with horror. I had myself suffered, even in my decent second-cabin berth, from the lack of air; and as the night promised to be fine and quiet, I determined to sleep on deck, and advised all who complained of their quarters to follow my example. I daresay a dozen of others agreed to do so, and I thought we should have been quite a party.

Yet, when I brought up my rug about seven bells, there was no one to be seen but the watch. That chimerical terror of good night-air, which makes men close their windows, list their doors, and seal themselves up with their own poisonous exhalations, had sent all these healthy workmen down below. One would think we had been brought up in a fever country ; yet in England the most malarious districts are in the bedchambers.

I felt saddened at this defection, and yet half-pleased to have the night so quietly to myself. The wind had hauled a little ahead on the starboard bow, and was dry but chilly. I found a shelter near the fire-hole, and made myself snug for the night. The ship moved over the uneven sea with a gentle and cradling movement. The ponderous, organic labours of the engine in her bowels occupied the mind, and prepared

it for slumber. From time to time a
heavier lurch would disturb me as I lay,
and recall me to the obscure borders of
consciousness ; or I heard, as it were
through a veil, the clear note of the
clapper on the brass and the beautiful
sea-cry, 'All 's well ! ' I know nothing,
whether for poetry or music, that can
surpass the effect of these two syllables
in the darkness of a night at sea.

The day dawned fairly enough, and
during the early part we had some pleasant hours to improve acquaintance in
the open air ; but towards nightfall the
wind freshened, the rain begin to fall,
and the sea rose so high that it was
difficult to keep one's footing on the
deck. I have spoken of our concerts.
We were indeed a musical ship's company, and cheered our way into exile
with the fiddle, the accordion, and the
songs of all nations. Good, bad, or
indifferent — Scottish, English, Irish,

Russian, German or Norse,— the songs
were received with generous applause.
Once or twice, a recitation, very spirit-
edly rendered in a powerful Scottish
accent, varied the proceedings; and
once we sought in vain to dance a quadrille, eight men of us together, to the
music of the violin.   The performers
were all humorous, frisky fellows, who
loved to cut capers in private life; but
as soon as they were arranged for the
dance, they conducted themselves like
so many mutes at a funeral. I have
never seen decorum pushed so far; and
as this was not expected, the quadrille
was soon whistled down, and the dancers departed under a cloud. Eight
Frenchmen, even eight Englishmen
from another rank of society, would
have dared to make some fun for themselves and the spectators; but the working man, when sober, takes an extreme
and even melancholy view of personal

deportment. A fifth-form schoolboy
is not more careful of dignity. He
dares not be comical; his fun must escape from him unprepared, and above
all, it must be unaccompanied by any
physical demonstration. I like his society under most circumstances, but let
me never again join with him in public
gambols.

But the impulse to sing was strong,
and triumphed over modesty and even
the inclemencies of sea and sky. On
this rough Saturday night, we got together by the main deck-house, in a
place sheltered from the wind and rain.
Some clinging to a ladder which led to
the hurricane deck, and the rest knitting
arms or taking hands, we made a ring
to support the women in the violent
lurching of the ship; and when we were
thus disposed, sang to our hearts' content. Some of the songs were appropriate to the scene; others strikingly

the reverse.   Bastard doggrel of the
music-hall, such as, 'Around her splendid form, I weaved the magic circle,'
sounded bald, bleak, and pitifully silly.
'We don't want to fight, but, by Jingo,
if we do,' was in some measure saved by
the vigour and unanimity with which
the chorus was thrown forth into the
night.   I observed a Platt-Deutsch
mason, entirely innocent of English,
adding heartily to the general effect.
And perhaps the German mason is but
a fair example of the sincerity with
which the song was rendered ; for nearly
all with whom I conversed upon the
subject were bitterly opposed to war,
and attributed their own misfortunes,
and frequently their own taste for
whisky, to the campaigns in Zululand
and Afghanistan.

Every now and again, however, some
song that touched the pathos of our sit-

uation was given forth ; and you could
hear by the voices that took up the bur-
den how the sentiment came home to
each. 'The Anchor's Weighed' was
true for us. We were indeed 'Rocked
on the bosom of the stormy deep.'
How many of us could say with the
singer, 'I'm lonely to-night, love, without you,' or 'Go, some one, and tell
them from me, to write me a letter from
home!' And when was there a more
appropriate moment for 'Auld Lang
Syne' than now, when the land, the
friends, and the affections of that
mingled but beloved time were fading
and fleeing behind us in the vessel's
wake? It pointed forward to the hour
when these labours should be overpast,
to the return voyage, and to many a
meeting in the sanded inn, when those
who had parted in the spring of youth
should again drink a cup of kindness in

their age. Had not Burns contemplated emigration, I scarce believe he would have found that note.

All Sunday the weather remained wild and cloudy; many were prostrated by sickness; only five sat down to tea in the second cabin, and two of these departed abruptly ere the meal was at an end. The Sabbath was observed strictly by the majority of the emigrants. I heard an old woman express her surprise that 'the ship didna gae doon,' as she saw some one pass her with a chess-board on the holy day. Some sang Scottish psalms. Many went to service, and in true Scottish fashion came back ill pleased with their divine. 'I didna think he was an experienced preacher,' said one girl to me.

It was a bleak, uncomfortable day; but at night, by six bells, although the wind had not yet moderated, the clouds were all wrecked and blown away behind

the rim of the horizon, and the stars
came out thickly overhead.   I saw Venus
burning as steadily and sweetly across
this hurly-burly of the winds and waters
as ever at home upon the summer woods.
The engine pounded, the screw tossed
out of the water with a roar, and shook
the ship from end to end; the bows
battled with loud reports against the
billows: and as I stood in the lee-scup-
pers and looked up to where the funnel
leaned out, over my head, vomiting
smoke, and the black and monstrous
tops ils blotted, at each lurch, a different crop of stars, it seemed as if all this
trouble were a thing of small account,
and that just above the mast reigned
peace unbroken and eternal.

Steerage Scenes

OUR companion (Steerage No. 2 and 3) was a favourite resort. Down one flight of stairs there was a comparatively large open space, the center occupied by a hatchway, which made a convenient seat for about twenty persons, while barrels, coils of rope, and the carpenter's bench afforded perches for perhaps as many more. The canteen, or steerage bar, was on one side of the stair; on the other, a no less attractive spot, the cabin of the indefatigable interpreter. I have seen people packed into this space like herrings in a barrel, and many merry evenings prolonged there until five bells, when the lights were ruthlessly extinguished and all must go to roost.

It had been rumoured since Friday
that there was a fiddler aboard, who lay
sick and unmelodious in Steerage No.
1; and on the Monday forenoon, as I
came down the companion, I was saluted
by something in Strathspey time. A
white-faced Orpheus was cheerily playing to an audience of white-faced women.
It was as much as he could do to play,
and some of his hearers were scarce able
to sit; yet they had crawled from their
bunks at the first experimental flourish,
and found better than medicine in the
music. Some of the heaviest heads
began to nod in time, and a degree of
animation looked from some of the pal-
est eyes. Humanly speaking, it is a
more important matter to play the fiddle, even badly, than to write huge
works upon recondite subjects. What
could Mr. Darwin have done for these
sick women? But this fellow scraped
away; and the world was positively a

better place for all who heard him. We
have yet to understand the economical
value of these mere accomplishments.
I told the fiddler he was a happy man,
carrying happiness about with him in
his fiddle-case, and he seemed alive to
the fact.

'It is a privilege,' I said. He thought
a while upon the word, turning it over
in his Scots head, and then answered
with conviction, 'Yes, a privilege.'

That night I was summoned by 'Merrily danced the Quaker's wife' into the
companion of Steerage No. 4 and 5.
This was, properly speaking, but a strip
across a deck-house, lit by a sickly lantern which swung to and fro with the
motion of the ship. Through the open
slide-door we had a glimpse of a grey
night sea, with patches of phosphores-
cent foam flying, swift as birds, into the
wake, and the horizon rising and falling
as the vessel rolled to the wind. In the

center the companion ladder plumped
down sheerly like an open pit.   Below,
on the first landing, and lighted by
another lamp, lads and lasses danced,
not more than three at a time for lack of
space, in jigs and reels and hornpipes.
Above, on either side, there was a recess
railed with iron, perhaps two feet wide
and four long, which stood for orchestra
and seats of honour.   In the one bal-
cony, five slatternly Irish lasses sat
woven in a comely group.   In the other
was posted Orpheus, his body, which
was convulsively in motion, forming an
odd contrast to his somnolent, imper-
turbable Scots face.   His brother, a dark
man with a vehement, interested coun-
tenance, who made a god of the fiddler,
sat by with open mouth, drinking in the
general admiration and throwing out
remarks to kindle it.

'That's a bonny hornpipe now,' he
would say, 'it's a great favourite with

performers; they dance the sand dance
to it.' And he expounded the sand
dance. Then suddenly, it would be a
long 'Hush!' with uplifted finger and
glowing, supplicating eyes; 'he's going
to play "Auld Robin Gray" on one
string!' And throughout this excruciat-
ing movement, — 'On one string, that's
on one string!' he kept crying. I
would have given something myself that
it had been on none; but the hearers
were much awed. I called for a tune or
two, and thus introduced myself to the
notice of the brother, who directed his
talk to me for some little while, keeping,
I need hardly mention, true to his topic,
like the seamen to the star. 'He's
grand of it,' he said confidentially.
'His master was a music-hall man.'
Indeed the music-hall man had left his
mark, for our fiddler was ignorant of
many of our best old airs; 'Logie o'
Buchan,' for instance, he only knew as a

4

quick, jigging figure in a set of qua-
drilles, and had never heard it called by
name.   Perhaps, after all, the brother
was the more interesting performer of
the two.   I have spoken with him afterwards repeatedly, and found him always
the same quick, fiery bit of a man, not
without brains; but he never showed to
such advantage as when he was thus
squiring the fiddler into public note.
There is nothing more becoming than
a genuine admiration; and it shares this
with love, that it does not become contemptible although misplaced.

The dancing was but feebly carried
on.   The space was almost impractic-
ably small; and the Irish wenches combined the extreme of bashfulness about
this innocent display with a surprising
impudence and roughness of address.
Most often, either the fiddle lifted up
its voice unheeded, or only a couple
of lads would be footing it and snap-

ping fingers on the landing. And such
was the eagerness of the brother to display all the acquirements of his idol,
and such the sleepy indifference of the
performer, that the tune would as often
as not be changed, and the hornpipe
expire into a ballad before the dancers
had cut half a dozen shuffles.

In the meantime, however, the audience had been growing more and more
numerous every moment; there was
hardly standing-room round the top of
the companion; and the strange
instinct of the race moved some of the
new-comers to close both the doors, so
that the atmosphere grew insupportable.
It was a good place, as the saying is, to
leave.

The wind hauled ahead with a head
sea. By ten at night heavy sprays were
flying and drumming over the forecastle; the companion of Steerage No.
1 had to be closed, and the door of

communication through the second
cabin thrown open. Either from the
convenience of the opportunity, or
because we had already a number of
acquaintances in that part of the ship,
Mr. Jones and I paid it a late visit.
Steerage No. 1 is shaped like an isos-
celes triangle, the sides opposite the
equal angles bulging outward with the
contour of the ship. It is lined with
eight pens of sixteen bunks apiece, four
bunks below and four above on either
side. At night the place is lit with two
lanterns, one to each table. As the
steamer beat on her way among the
rough billows, the light passed through
violent phases of change, and was
thrown to and fro and up and down
with startling swiftness. You were
tempted to wonder, as you looked, how
so thin a glimmer could control and
disperse such solid blackness. When
Jones and I entered we found a little

company of our acquaintances seated together at the triangular foremost table. A more forlorn party, in more dismal circumstances, it would be hard to imagine. The motion here in the ship's nose was very violent; the uproar of the sea often overpoweringly loud. The yellow flicker of the lantern spun round and round and tossed the shadows in masses. The air was hot, but it struck a chill from its fœtor. From all round in the dark bunks, the scarcely human noises of the sick joined into a kind of farmyard chorus. In the midst, these five friends of mine were keeping up what heart they could in company. Singing was their refuge from discomfortable thoughts and sensations. One piped, in feeble tones, 'Oh why left I my hame?' which seemed a pertinent question in the circumstances. Another, from the invisible horrors of a pen where he lay

dog-sick upon the upper shelf, found
courage, in a blink of his sufferings, to
give us several verses of the 'Death of
Nelson'; and it was odd and eerie to
hear the chorus breathe feebly from all
sorts of dark corners, and 'this day has
done his dooty' rise and fall and be
taken up again in this dim *inferno*, to
an accompaniment of plunging, hollow-
sounding bows and the rattling spray-
showers overhead.

All seemed unfit for conversation; a
certain dizziness had interrupted the
activity of their minds; and except to
sing they were tongue-tied. There was
present, however, one tall, powerful
fellow of doubtful nationality, being
neither quite Scotsman nor altogether
Irish, but of surprising clearness of
conviction on the highest problems.
He had gone nearly beside himself on
the Sunday, because of a general back-
wardness to indorse his definition of

mind as 'a living, thinking substance
which cannot be felt, heard, or seen '—
nor, I presume, although he failed to
mention it, smelt. Now he came forward in a pause with another contribu-
tion to our culture.

'Just by way of change,' said he, I 'll
ask you a Scripture riddle. There 's
profit in them too,' he added ungram-
matically.

This was the riddle—

  ' C and P
  Did agree
  To cut down C ;
  But C and P
  Could not agree
  Without the leave of G
  All the people cried to see
  The crueltie
  Of C and P.'

Harsh are the words of Mercury after
the songs of Apollo! We were a long
while over the problem, shaking our
heads and gloomily wondering how a

man could be such a fool; but at length
he put us out of suspense and divulged
the fact that C and P stood for Caiaphas
and Pontius Pilate.

I think it must have been the riddle
that settled us; but the motion and the
close air likewise hurried our departure.
We had not been gone long, we heard
next morning, ere two or even three
out of the five fell sick.   We thought it
little wonder on the whole, for the sea
kept contrary all night.   I now made
my bed upon the second cabin floor,
where, although I ran the risk of being
stepped upon, I had a free current of
air, more or less vitiated indeed, and
running only from steerage to steerage,
but at least not stagnant; and from this
couch, as well as the usual sounds of a
rough night at sea, the hateful cough-
ing and retching of the sick and the
sobs of children, I heard a man run
wild with terror beseeching his friend

for encouragement. 'The ship's going down!' he cried with a thrill of agony. 'The ship's going down!' he repeated, now in a blank whisper, now with his voice rising towards a sob; and his friend might reassure him, reason with him, joke at him—all was in vain, and the old cry came back, 'The ship's going down!' There was something panicy and catching in the emotion of his tones; and I saw in a clear flash what an involved and hideous tragedy was a disaster to an emigrant ship. If this whole parishful of people came no more to land, into how many houses would the newspaper carry woe, and what a great part of the web of our corporate human life would be rent across for ever!

The next morning when I came on deck I found a new world indeed. The wind was fair; the sun mounted into a cloudless heaven; through great dark blue seas the ship cut a swathe of curded foam. The horizon was dotted all day with companionable sails, and the sun shone pleasantly on the long, heaving deck.

We had many fine-weather diversions to beguile the time. There was a single chess-board and a single pack of cards. Sometimes as many as twenty of us would be playing dominoes for love. Feats of dexterity, puzzles for the intelligence, some arithmetical, some of the same order as the old problem of the fox and goose and cabbage, were always welcome; and the latter, I observed, more popular as well as more conspicuously well done than the former. We had a regular daily competition to guess the vessel's progress; and twelve o'clock, when the result was published in the wheel-house, came to be a moment of considerable interest. But the interest was unmixed. Not a bet was laid upon

our guesses. From the Clyde to Sandy
Hook I never heard a wager offered or
taken. We had, besides, romps in
plenty. Puss in the Corner, which we
had rebaptized, in more manly style,
Devil and four Corners, was my own
favorite game; but there were many
who preferred another, the humor of
which was to box a person's ears until
he found out who had cuffed him.

This Tuesday morning we were all
delighted with the change of weather,
and in the highest possible spirits. We
got in a cluster like bees, sitting between each other's feet under lee of the
deck-houses. Stories and laughter went
around. The children climbed about
the shrouds. White faces appeared for
the first time, and began to take on
colour from the wind. I was kept hard
at work making cigarettes for one amateur after another, and my less than
moderate skill was heartily admired.

Lastly, down sat the fiddler in our midst and began to discourse his reels, and jigs, and ballads, with now and then a voice or two to take up the air and throw in the interest of human speech.

Through this merry and good-hearted scene there came three cabin passengers, a gentleman and two young ladies, picking their way with little gracious titters of indulgence, and a Lady-Bountiful air about nothing, which galled me to the quick.   I have little of the radical in social questions, and have always nourished an idea that one person was as good as another.   But I began to be troubled by this episode.   It was astonishing what insults these people managed to convey by their presence. They seemed to throw their clothes in our faces.   Their eyes searched us all over for tatters and incongruities.   A laugh was ready at their lips ; but they were too well-mannered to indulge it in

our hearing. Wait a bit, till they were
all back in the saloon, and then hear
how wittily they would depict the manners of the steerage. We were in truth
very innocently, cheerfully, and sensibly
engaged, and there was no shadow of
excuse for the swaying elegant superiority with which these damsels passed
among us, or for the stiff and waggish
glances of their squire. Not a word was
said ; only when they were gone Mackay sullenly damned their impudence
under his breath ; but we were all con-
scious of an icy influence and a dead
break in the course of our enjoyment.

Steerage Types

W E had a fellow on board, an Irish-
American, for all the world like
a beggar in a print by Callot ; one-eyed,
with great, splay crow's-feet round the
sockets ; a knotty squab nose coming
down over his mustache ; a miraculous
hat ; a shirt that had been white, ay,
ages long ago ; an alpaca coat in its
last sleeves ; and, without hyperbole, no
buttons to his trousers.   Even in these
rags and tatters, the man twinkled all
over with impudence like a piece of
sham jewellery ; and I have heard him
offer a situation to one of his fellow-
passengers with the air of a lord.   Nothing could overlie such a fellow ; a kind
of base success was written on his brow.
He was then in his ill days ; but I can

57

imagine him in Congress with his mouth
full of bombast and sawder. As we
moved in the same circle, I was brought
necessarily into his society. I do not
think I ever heard him say anything
that was true, kind, or interesting ; but
there was entertainment in the man's
demeanour. You might call him a
half-educated Irish Tigg.

Our Russian made a remarkable contrast to this impossible fellow. Rumours
and legends were current in the steerages about his antecedents. Some said
he was a Nihilist escaping ; others set
him down for a harmless spendthrift,
who had squandered fifty thousand rou-
bles, and whose father had now des-
patched him to America by way of pen-
ance. Either tale might flourish in
security ; there was no contradiction to
be feared, for the hero spoke not one
word of English. I got on with him
lumberingly enough in broken German,

and learnt from his own lips that he had
been an apothecary. He carried the
photograph of his betrothed in a
pocket-book, and remarked that it did
not do her justice. The cut of his head
stood out from among the passengers
with an air of startling strangeness.
The first natural instinct was to take
him for a desperado ; but although the
features, to our Western eyes, had a
barbaric and unhomely cast, the eye
both reassured and touched. It was
large and very dark and soft, with an
expression of dumb endurance, as if it
had often looked on desperate circumstances and never looked on them without resolution.

He cried out when I used the word.
'No, no,' he said, ' not resolution.'

'The resolution to endure,' I explained.

And then he shrugged his shoulders,
and said, '*Ach, ja,*' with gusto, like a

5

man who has been flattered in his favourite pretensions. Indeed, he was always hinting at some secret sorrow; and his life, he said, had been one of unusual trouble and anxiety ; so the legends of the steerage may have represented at least some shadow of the truth. Once, and once only, he sang a song at our concerts; standing forth without embarrassment, his great stature somewhat humped, his long arms frequently extended, his Kalmuck head thrown backward. It was a suitable piece of music, as deep as a cow's bellow and wild like the White Sea. He was struck and charmed by the freedom and sociality of our manners. At home, he said, no one on a journey would speak to him, but those with whom he would not care to speak ; thus unconsciously involving himself in the condemnation of his countrymen. But Russia was soon to be changed ; the ice

of the Neva was softening under the sun
of civilization; the new ideas, '*wie ein
feines violin,*' were audible among the
big empty drum notes of Imperial
diplomacy; and he looked to see a
great revival, though with a somewhat
indistinct and childish hope.

We had a father and son who made a
pair of Jacks-of-all-trades. It was the
son who sang the 'Death of Nelson'
under such contrarious circumstances.
He was by trade a shearer of ship
plates; but he could touch the organ,
had led two choirs, and played the flute
and piccolo in a professional string
band. His repertory of songs was,
besides, inexhaustible, and ranged im-
partially from the very best to the very
worst within his reach. Nor did he
seem to make the least distinction
between these extremes, but would
cheerfully follow up 'Tom Bowling'
with 'Around her splendid form.'

The father, an old, cheery, small piece of manhood, could do everything connected with tinwork from one end of the process to the other, use almost every carpenter's tool, and make picture frames to boot. 'I sat down with silver plate every Sunday,' said he, 'and pictures on the wall. I have made enough money to be rolling in my carriage. But, sir,' looking at me unsteadily with his bright rheumy eyes, 'I was troubled with a drunken wife.' He took a hostile view of matrimony in consequence. 'It's an old saying,' he remarked: 'God made 'em, and the devil he mixed 'em.'

I think he was justified by his experience. It was a dreary story. He would bring home three pounds on Saturday, and on Monday all the clothes would be in pawn. Sick of the useless struggle, he gave up a paying contract, and contended himself with small and ill-

paid jobs. 'A bad job was as good as
a good job for me,' he said; 'it all went
the same way.' Once the wife showed
signs of amendment; she kept steady
for weeks on end; it was again worth
while to labour and to do one's best.
The husband found a good situation
some distance from home, and, to make
a little upon every hand, started the
wife in a cook-shop; the children were
here and there, busy as mice; savings
began to grow together in the bank, and
the golden age of hope had returned
again to that unhappy family. But one
week my old acquaintance, getting
earlier through with his work, came
home on the Friday instead of the Saturday, and there was his wife to receive
him reeling drunk. He 'took and
gave her a pair o' black eyes,' for which
I pardon him, nailed up the cook-shop
door, gave up his situation, and resigned
himself to a life of poverty, with the

workhouse at the end.   As the children came to their full age they fled the house, and established themselves in other countries; some did well, some not so well ; but the father remained at home alone with his drunken wife, all his sound-hearted pluck and varied accomplishments depressed and nega-tived.

Was she dead now ? or, after all these years, had he broken the chain, and run from home like a schoolboy ?   I could not discover which ; but here at least he was out on the adventure, and still one of the bravest and most youthful men on board.

'Now, I suppose, I must put my old bones to work again,' said he; 'but I can do a turn yet.'

And the son to whom he was going, I asked, was he not able to support him?

' Oh yes,' he replied.   ' But I 'm never happy without a job on hand.   And

I'm stout ; I can eat a'most anything.
You see no craze about me.'

This tale of a drunken wife was paral-
leled on board by another of a drunken
father. He was a capable man, with a
good chance in life ; but he had drunk
up two thriving businesses like a bottle
of sherry, and involved his sons along
with him in ruin. Now they were on
board with us, fleeing his disastrous
neighbourhood.

Total abstinence, like all ascetical
conclusions, is unfriendly to the most
generous, cheerful, and human parts of
man ; but it could have adduced many
instances and arguments from among
our ship's company. I was one day
conversing with a kind and happy
Scotsman, running to fat and perspira-
tion in the physical, but with a taste for
poetry and a genial sense of fun. I had
asked him his hopes in emigrating.
They were like those of so many others,

vague and unfounded ; times were bad
at home ; they were said to have a turn
for the better in the States ; and a man
could get on anywhere, he thought.
That was precisely the weak point of his
position ; for if he could get on in
America, why could he not do the same
in Scotland ? But I never had the
courage to use that argument, though it
was often on the tip of my tongue, and
instead I agreed with him heartily, adding, with reckless originality, 'If the
man stuck to his work, and kept away
from drink.'

'Ah!' said he slowly, 'the drink!
You see, that 's just my trouble.'

He spoke with a simplicity that was
touching, looking at me at the same
time with something strange and timid
in his eye, half-ashamed, half-sorry, like
a good child who knows he should be
beaten.   You would have said he recognized a destiny to which he was born,

and accepted the consequences mildly.
Like the merchant Abudah, he was
at the same time fleeing from his
destiny and carrying it along with
him, the whole at an expense of six
guineas.

As far as I saw, drink, idleness, and
incompetency were the three great
causes of emigration, and for all of
them, and drink first and foremost, this
trick of getting transported overseas
appears to me the silliest means of cure.
You cannot run away from a weakness;
you must some time fight it out or
perish; and if that be so, why not now,
and where you stand? *Cælum non ani-
mam.* Change Glenlivat for Bourbon,
and it is still whisky, only not so good.
A sea-voyage will not give a man the
nerve to put aside cheap pleasure; emigration has to be done before we climb
the vessel; an aim in life is the only
fortune worth the finding; and it is not

to be found in foreign lands, but in the heart itself.

Speaking generally, there is no vice of this kind more contemptible than another; for each is but a result and outward sign of a soul tragically shipwrecked. In the majority of cases, cheap pleasure is resorted to by way of anodyne. The pleasure-seeker sets forth upon life with high and difficult ambitions; he meant to be nobly good and nobly happy, though at as little pains as possible to himself; and it is because all has failed in his celestial enterprise that you now behold him rolling in the garbage. Hence the comparative success of the teetotal pledge; because to a man who had nothing it sets at least a negative aim in life. Somewhat as prisoners beguile their days by taming a spider, the reformed drunkard makes an interest out of abstaining from intoxicating drinks, and may live for that negation. There is something, at least, *not to be done* each day ; and a cold triumph awaits him every evening.

We had one on board with us, whom I have already referred to under the name of Mackay, who seemed to me not only a good instance of this failure in life of which we have been speaking, but a good type of the intelligence which here surrounded me. Physically he was a small Scotsman, standing a little back as though he were already carrying the elements of a corporation, and his looks somewhat marred by the smallness of his eyes. Mentally, he was endowed above the average. There were but few subjects on which he could not converse with understanding and a dash of wit; delivering himself slowly and with gusto, like a man who enjoyed his own sententiousness. He was a dry, quick, pertinent debater, speaking

with a small voice, and swinging on his
heels to launch and emphasize an argument. When he began a discussion,
he could not bear to leave it off, but
would pick the subject to the bone,
without once relinquishing a point. An
engineer by trade, Mackay believed in
the unlimited perfectibility of all ma-
chines except the human machine. The
latter he gave up with ridicule for a
compound of carrion and perverse
gases. He had an appetite for disconnected facts which I can only compare
to the savage taste for beads. What is
called information was indeed a passion
with the man, and he not only delighted
to receive it, but could pay you back in
kind.

With all these capabilities, here was
Mackay, already no longer young, on
his way to a new country, with no pros-
pects, no money, and but little hope.
He was almost tedious in the cynical

disclosures of his despair. 'The ship
may go down for me,' he would say,
'now or to-morrow. I have nothing to
lose and nothing to hope.' And again ;
'I am sick of the whole damned performance.' He was, like the kind little
man already quoted, another so-called
victim of the bottle. But Mackay was
miles from publishing his weakness to
the world; laid the blame of his failure
on corrupt masters and a corrupt State
policy ; and after he had been one night
overtaken and had played the buffoon
in his cups, sternly, though not without
tact, suppressed all reference to his es-
capade. It was a treat to see him man-
age this ; the various jesters withered
under his gaze, and you were forced to
recognize in him a certain steely force,
and a gift of command which might
have ruled a senate.

In truth it was not whisky that had
ruined him ; he was ruined long before

for all good human purposes but conversation. His eyes were sealed by a
cheap, school-book materialism. He
could see nothing in the world but
money and steam-engines. He did not
know what you meant by the word happiness. He had forgotten the simple
emotions of childhood, and perhaps
never encountered the delights of youth.
He believed in production, that useful
figment of economy, as if it had been
real like laughter ; and production,
without prejudice to liquor, was his god
and guide. One day he took me to
task — a novel cry to me — upon the
over-payment of literature. Literary
men, he said, were more highly paid
than artisans ; yet the artisan made
threshing-machines and butter-churns,
and the man of letters, except in the
way of a few useful handbooks, made
nothing worth the while. He produced
a mere fancy article. Mackay's notion

of a book was *Hoppus's Measurer*. Now
in my time I have possessed and even
studied that work ; but if I were to be
left to-morrow on Juan Fernandez,
Hoppus's is not the book that I should
choose for my companion volume.

I tried to fight the point with Mackay.
I made him own that he had taken
pleasure in reading books otherwise, to
his view, insignificant ; but he was too
wary to advance a step beyond the
admission. It was in vain for me to
argue that here was pleasure ready-made
and running from the spring, whereas
his ploughs and butter-churns were but
means and mechanisms to give men the
necessary food and leisure before they
start upon the search for pleasure ; he
jibbed and ran away from such conclusions. The thing was different, he
declared, and nothing was serviceable
but what had to do with food. 'Eat,
eat, eat!' he cried ; 'that's the bottom

and the top.' By an odd irony of circumstance, he grew so much interested in this discussion that he let the hour slip by unnoticed and had to go without his tea. He had enough sense and humour, indeed he had no lack of either, to have chuckled over this himself in private; and even to me he referred to it with the shadow of a smile.

Mackay was a hot bigot. He would not hear of religion. I have seen him waste hours of time in argument with all sort of poor human creatures who understood neither him nor themselves, and he had had the boyishness to dissect and criticise even so small a matter as the riddler's definition of mind. He snorted aloud with zealotry and the lust for intellectual battle. Anything, whatever it was, that seemed to him likely to discourage the continued passionate production of corn and steam-engines he resented like a conspiracy against the people. Thus, when I put in the plea for literature, that it was only in good books, or in the society of the good, that a man could get help in his conduct, he declared I was in a different world from him. 'Damn my conduct!' said he. 'I have given it up for a bad job. My question is, 'Can I drive a nail?' And he plainly looked upon me as one who was insidiously seeking to reduce the people's annual bellyful of corn and steam-engines.

It may be argued that these opinions spring from the defect of culture; that a narrow and pinching way of life not only exaggerates to a man the importance of material conditions, but indirectly, by denying him the necessary books and leisure, keeps his mind ignorant of larger thoughts; and that hence springs this overwhelming concern about diet, and hence the bald view of existence professed by Mackay. Had

6

this been an English peasant the conclusion would be tenable. But Mackay
had most of the elements of a liberal
education. He had skirted metaphysi-
cal and mathematical studies. He had
a thoughtful hold of what he knew,
which would be exceptional among
bankers. He had been brought up in
the midst of hot-house piety, and told,
with incongruous pride, the story of his
own brother's deathbed ecstasies. Yet
he had somehow failed to fulfil himself,
and was adrift like a dead thing among
external circumstances, without hope or
lively preference or shaping aim. And
further, there seemed a tendency among
many of his fellows to fall into the same
blank and unlovely opinions. One
thing, indeed, is not to be learned in
Scotland, and that is the way to be
happy. Yet that is the whole of culture,
and perhaps two-thirds of morality.
Can it be that the Puritan school, by

divorcing a man from nature, by thinning out his instincts, and setting a stamp of its disapproval on whole fields of human activity and interest, leads at last directly to material greed ?

Nature is a good guide through life, and the love of simple pleasures next, if not superior, to virtue; and we had on board an Irishman who based his claim to the widest and most affectionate popularity precisely upon these two qualities, that he was natural and happy. He boasted a fresh colour, a tight little figure, unquenchable gaiety, and indefatigable good-will. His clothes puzzled the diagnostic mind, until you heard he had been once a private coachman, when they became eloquent and seemed a part of his biography. His face contained the rest, and, I fear, a prophecy of the future; the hawk's nose above accorded so ill with the pink baby's mouth below. His spirit and his pride belonged, you

might say, to the nose ; while it was the
general shiftlessness expressed by the
other that had thrown him from situation to situation, and at length on board
the emigrant ship.   Barney ate, so to
speak, nothing from the galley ; his own
tea, butter and eggs supported him
throughout the voyage ; and about meal-
time you might often find him up to the
elbows in amateur cookery.   His was
the first voice heard singing among all
the passengers ; he was the first who fell
to dancing.   From Loch Foyle to Sandy
Hook, there was not a piece of fun
undertaken but there was Barney in the
midst.

You ought to have seen him when he
stood up to sing at our concerts—his tight
little figure stepping to and fro, and
his feet shuffling to the air, his eyes seeking and bestowing encouragement—and
to have enjoyed the bow, so nicely calculated between jest and earnest, between

grace and clumsiness, with which he brought each song to a conclusion. He was not only a great favourite among ourselves, but his songs attracted the lords of the saloon, who often leaned to hear him over the rails of the hurricane-deck. He was somewhat pleased, but not at all abashed by this attention; and one night, in the midst of his famous performance of 'Billy Keogh,' I saw him spin half round in a pirouette and throw an audacious wink to an old gentleman above.

This was the more characteristic, as, for all his daffing, he was a modest and very polite little fellow among ourselves.

He would not have hurt the feelings of a fly, nor throughout the passage did he give a shadow of offense; yet he was always, by his innocent freedoms and love of fun, brought upon that narrow margin where politeness must be natural to walk without a fall. He was once

seriously angry, and that in a grave,
quiet manner, because they supplied no
fish on Friday; for Barney was a con-
scientious Catholic. He had likewise
strict notions of refinement; and when,
late one evening, after the women had
retired, a young Scotsman struck up an
indecent song, Barney's drab clothes
were immediately missing from the
group. His taste was for the society of
gentlemen, of whom, with the reader's
permission, there was no lack in our five
steerages and second cabin; and he
avoided the rough and positive with a
girlish shrinking. Mackay, partly from
his superior powers of mind, which rendered him incomprehensible, partly from
his extreme opinions, was especially dis-
tasteful to the Irishman. I have seen
him slink off with backward looks of
terror and offended delicacy, while the
other, in his witty, ugly way, had been

professing hostility to God, and an
extreme theatrical readiness to be shipwrecked on the spot. These utterances
hurt the little coachman's modesty like
a bad word.

The Sick Man

ONE night Jones, the young O'Reilly, and myself were walking arm-in-arm and briskly up and down the deck. Six bells had rung ; a head-wind blew chill and fitful, the fog was closing in with a sprinkle of rain, and the fog-whistle had been turned on, and now divided time with its unwelcome outcries, loud like a bull, thrilling and intense like a mosquito. Even the watch lay somewhere snugly out of sight.

For some time we observed something lying black and huddled in the scuppers, which at last heaved a little and moaned aloud. We ran to the rails. An elderly man, but whether passenger or seaman it was impossible in the darkness to determine, lay grovel-

83

ling on his belly in the wet scuppers,
and kicking feebly with his outspread
toes. We asked him what was amiss,
and he replied incoherently, with a
strange accent and in a voice unmanned
by terror, that he had cramp in the
stomach, that he had been ailing all
day, had seen the doctor twice, and had
walked the deck against fatigue till he
was overmastered and had fallen where
we found him.

Jones remained by his side, while
O'Reilly and I hurried off to seek the
doctor. We knocked in vain at the
doctor's cabin; there came no reply;
nor could we find any one to guide us.
It was no time for delicacy; so we ran
once more forward; and I, whipping
up a ladder and touching my hat to the
officer of the watch, addressed him as
politely as I could :

'I beg your pardon, sir ; but there is
a man lying bad with cramp in the

lee scuppers; and I can't find the doctor.'

He looked at me peeringly in the darkness; and then, somewhat harshly, 'Well, *I* can't leave the bridge, my man,' said he.

'No, sir; but you can tell me what to do,' I returned.

'Is it one of the crew?' he asked.

'I believe him to be a fireman,' I replied.

I daresay officers are much annoyed by complaints and alarmist information from their freight of human creatures; but certainly, whether it was the idea that the sick man was one of the crew, or from something conciliatory in my address, the officer in question was immediately relieved and mollified ; and speaking in a voice much freer from constraint, advised me to find a steward and despatch him in quest of the doctor, who would now be in the smoking-room over his pipe.

One of the stewards was often enough
to be found about this hour down our
companion, Steerage No. 2 and 3; that
was his smoking-room of a night.   Let
me call him Blackwood.   O'Reilly and
I rattled down the companion, breathing hurry; and in his shirt-sleeves and
perched across the carpenter's bench
upon one thigh, found Blackwood; a
neat, bright, dapper, Glasgow-looking
man, with a bead of an eye and a rank
twang in his speech.   I forget who was
with him, but the pair were enjoying a
deliberate talk over their pipes.   I daresay he was tired with his day's work,
and eminently comfortable at that moment; and the truth is I did not stop
to consider his feelings, but told my
story in a breath.

'Steward,' said I, 'there's a man lying
bad with cramp, and I can't find the
doctor.'

He turned upon me as pert as a spar-

row, but with a black look that is the
prerogative of man ; and taking his pipe
out of his mouth—

'That's none of my business,' said
he. 'I don't care.'

I could have strangled the little ruf-
fian where he sat. The thought of his
cabin civility and cabin tips filled me
with indignation. I glanced at O'Reilly ;
he was pale and quivering, and looked
like assault and battery, every inch of
him. But we had a better card than
violence.

'You will have to make it your business,' said I, 'for I am sent to you by
the officer on the bridge.'

Blackwood was fairly tripped. He
made no answer, but put out his pipe,
gave me one murderous look, and set
off upon his errand strolling. From
that day forward, I should say, **he**
improved to me in courtesy, as though
he had repented his evil speech and

were anxious to leave a better impression.

When we got on deck again, Jones was still beside the sick man; and two or three late stragglers had gathered round and were offering suggestions. One proposed to give the patient water, which was promptly negatived. Another bade us hold him up; he himself prayed to be let lie; but as it was at least as well to keep him off the streaming decks, O'Reilly and I supported him between us. It was only by main force that we did so, and neither an easy nor an agreeable duty; for he fought in his paroxysms like a frightened child, and moaned miserably when he resigned himself to our control.

'O let me lie!' he pleaded. 'I'll no' get better anyway.' And then, with a moan that went to my heart, 'O why did I come upon this miserable journey?'

I was reminded of the song which I had heard a little while before in the close, tossing steerage ; 'O why left I my hame ?'

Meantime Jones, relieved of his immediate charge, had gone off to the galley, where we could see a light.   There he found a belated cook scouring pans by the radiance of two lanterns, and one of these he sought to borrow.   The scullion was backward.   'Was it one of the crew ?' he asked.   And when Jones, smitten with my theory, had assured that it was a fireman, he reluctantly left his scouring and came towards us at an easy pace, with one of the lanterns swinging from his finger.   The light, as it reached the spot, showed us an elderly man, thick-set, and grizzled with years ; but the shifting and coarse shadows concealed from us the expression and even the design of his face.

So soon as the cook set eyes on him he gave a sort of whistle.

'*It's only a passenger!*' said he; and turning about, made, lantern and all, for the galley.

'He's a man anyway,' cried Jones in indignation.

'Nobody said he was a woman,' said a gruff voice, which I recognised for that of the bo's'un.

All this while there was no word of Blackwood or the doctor ; and now the officer came to our side of the ship and asked, over the hurricane-deck rails, if the doctor were not yet come.   We told him not.

'No ?' he repeated with a breathing of anger ; and we saw him hurry aft in person.

Ten minutes after the doctor made his appearance deliberately enough and examined our patient with the lantern.

He made little of the case, had the man
brought aft to the dispensary, dosed
him, and sent him forward to his bunk.
Two of his neighbours in the steerage
had now come to our assistance, express-
ing loud sorrow that such 'a fine cheery
body' should be sick; and these, claim-
ing a sort of possession, took him entirely under their own care. The drug
had probably relieved him, for he strug-
gled no more, and was led along plain-
tive and patient, but protesting. His
heart recoiled at the thought of the
steerage. 'O let me lie down upon the
bieldy side,' he cried; 'O dinna take
me down!' And again: 'O why did
ever I come upon this miserable voyage?' And yet once more, with a gasp
and a wailing prolongation of the fourth
word: 'I had no *call* to come.' But
there he was; and by the doctor's
orders and the kind force of his two
shipmates disappeared down the com-

7

panion of Steerage No. 1 into the den
allotted him.

At the foot of our own companion,
just where I found Blackwood, Jones
and the bo's'un were now engaged in
talk. This last was a gruff, cruel-look-
ing seaman, who must have passed near
half a century upon the seas; square-
headed, goat-bearded, with heavy blonde
eyebrows, and an eye without radiance,
but inflexibly steady and hard. I had not
forgotten his rough speech; but I re-
membered also that he had helped us
about the lantern; and now seeing him
in conversation with Jones, and being
choked with indignation, I proceeded
to blow off my steam.

'Well,' said I, 'I make you my com-
pliments upon your steward,' and furi-
ously narrated what had happened.

'I've nothing to do with him,' replied the bo's'un. 'They're all alike.
They wouldn't mind if they saw you

all lying dead one upon the top of another.'

This was enough. A very little humanity went a long way with me after the experience of the evening. A sympathy grew up at once between the bo's'un and myself; and that night, and during the next few days, I learned to appreciate him better. He was a remarkable type, and not at all the kind of man you find in books. He had been at Sebastopol under English colours; and again in a States ship, 'after the *Alabama*, and praying God we shouldn't find her.' He was a high Tory and a high Englishman. No manufacturer could have held opinions more hostile to the working man and his strikes. 'The workmen,' he said, 'think nothing of their country. They think of nothing but themselves. They're damned greedy, selfish fellows.' He would not hear of the decadence of

England. 'They say they send us beef from America,' he argued; 'but who pays for it? All the money in the world 's in England.' The Royal Navy was the best of possible services, according to him. 'Anyway the officers are gentlemen,' said he; 'and you can't get hazed to death by a damned non-commissioned ———— as you can in the army.' Among nations, England was the first; then came France. He respected the French navy and liked the French people; and if he were forced to make a new choice in life, 'by God, he would try Frenchmen!' For all his looks and rough, cold manners, I observed that children were never frightened by him; they divined him at once to be a friend; and one night when he had chalked his hand and went about stealthily setting his mark on people's clothes, it was incongruous to hear this formidable old salt chuckling over his boyish monkey trick.

In the morning, my first thought was of the sick man. I was afraid I should not recognise him, so baffling had been the light of the lantern ; and found myself unable to decide if he were Scots, English, or Irish. He had certainly employed north-country words and elisions; but the accent and the pronunciation seemed unfamiliar and incongruous in my ear.

To descend on an empty stomach into Steerage No. 1, was an adventure that required some nerve. The stench was atrocious; each respiration tasted in the throat like some horrible kind of cheese; and the squalid aspect of the place was aggravated by so many people worming themselves into their clothes in the twilight of the bunks. You may guess if I was pleased, not only for him, but for myself also, when I heard that

the sick man was better and had gone
on deck.

The morning was raw and foggy,
though the sun suffused the fog with
pink and amber; the fog-horn still
blew, stertorous and intermittent; and
to add to the discomfort, the seamen
were just beginning to wash down the
decks. But for a sick man this was
heaven compared to the steerage. I
found him standing on the hot-water
pipe, just forward of the saloon deck
house. He was smaller than I had fan-
cied, and plain-looking; but his face
was distinguished by strange and fasci-
nating eyes, limpid grey from a distance,
but, when looked into, full of changing
colours and grains of gold. His manners were mild and uncompromisingly
plain; and I soon saw that, when once
started, he delighted to talk. His accent and language had been formed in
the most natural way, since he was born

in Ireland, had lived a quarter of a century on the banks of Tyne, and was married to a Scots wife. A fisherman in the season, he had fished the east coast from Fisherrow to Whitby. When the season was over, and the great boats, which required extra hands, were once drawn up on shore till the next spring, he worked as a labourer about chemical furnaces, or along the wharves unloading vessels. In this comparatively humble way of life he had gathered a competence, and could speak of his comfortable house, his hayfield, and his garden. On this ship, where so many accomplished artisans were fleeing from starvation, he was present on a pleasure trip to visit a brother in New York.

Ere he started, he informed me, he had been warned against the steerage and the steerage fare, and recommended to bring with him a ham and tea and a spice loaf. But he laughed to scorn

such counsels. '*I'm* not afraid,' he had
told his adviser, '*I'll* get on for ten
days. I've not been a fisherman for
nothing.' For it is no light matter, as
he reminded me, to be in an open boat,
perhaps waist-deep with herrings, day
breaking with a scowl, and for miles on
every hand lee-shores, unbroken, iron-
bound, surf-beat, with only here and
there an anchorage where you dare not
lie, or a harbour impossible to enter
with the wind that blows. The life of
a North Sea fisher is one long chapter
of exposure and hard work and insufficient fare; and even if he makes land at
some bleak fisher port, perhaps the season is bad or his boat has been unlucky,
and after fifty hours' unsleeping vigi-
lance and toil, not a shop will give him
credit for a loaf of bread. Yet the
steerage of the emigrant ship had been
too vile for the endurance of a man
thus rudely trained. He had scarce

eaten since he came on board, until the
day before, when his appetite was tempted
by some excellent pea soup.   We were
all much of the same mind on board,
and beginning with myself, had dined
upon pea-soup not wisely but too well;
only with him the excess had been
punished, perhaps because he was weak-
ened by former abstinence, and his first
meal had resulted in a cramp.   He had
determined to live henceforth on biscuit; and when, two months later, he
should return to England, to make the
passage by saloon.   The second cabin,
after due inquiry, he scouted as another
edition of the steerage.

He spoke apologetically of his emotion when ill.   'Ye see, I had no call
to be here,' said he; 'and I thought it
was by with me last night.   I 've a good
house at home, and plenty to nurse me,
and I had no real call to leave them.'
Speaking of the attentions he had

received from his shipmates generally,
'they were all so kind,' he said, 'that
there 's none to mention.'   And except
in so far as I might share in this, he
troubled me with no reference to my
services.

But what affected me in the most
lively manner was the wealth of this
day-labourer, paying a two months'
pleasure visit to the States, and prepar-
ing to return in the saloon, and the new
testimony rendered by his story, not so
much to the horrors of the steerage as
to the habitual comfort of the working
classes.   One foggy, frosty December
evening, I encounted on Liberton Hill,
near Edinburgh, an Irish laborer trudg-
ing homeward from the fields.   Our
roads lay together, and it was natural
that we should fall into talk.   He was
covered with mud; an inoffensive, ignorant creature, who thought the Atlantic
Cable was a secret contrivance of the

masters the better to oppress labouring
mankind; and I confess I was astonished to learn that he had nearly three
hundred pounds in the bank. But this
man had travelled over most of the
world, and enjoyed wonderful opportunities on some American railroad, with
two dollars a shift and double pay on
Sunday and at night; whereas my fellow-passenger had never quitted Tyne-
side, and had made all that he possessed
in that same accursed, down-falling
England, whence skilled mechanics,
engineers, millwrights and carpenters
were fleeing as from the native country
of starvation.

Fitly enough, we slid off on the subject of strikes and wages and hard
times. Being from the Tyne, and a
man who had gained and lost in his
own pocket by these fluctuations, he
had much to say, and held strong opin-

ions on the subject.   He spoke sharply
of the masters, and, when I led him on,
of the men also.   The masters had been
selfish and obstructive; the men selfish,
silly, and light-headed.   He rehearsed
to me the course of a meeting at which
he had been present, and the somewhat
long discourse which he had there pro-
nounced, calling into question the wisdom and even the good faith of the
Union delegates; and although he had
escaped himself through flush times and
starvation times with a handsomely pro-
vided purse, he had so little faith in
either man or master, and so profound
a terror for the unerring Nemesis of
mercantile affairs, that he could think
of no hope for our country outside
of a sudden and complete political
subversion.   Down must go Lords
and Church and Army; and capital, by
some happy direction, must change

hands from worse to better, or England stood condemned. Such principles, he said, were growing 'like a seed.'

From this mild, soft, domestic man, these words sounded unusually ominous and grave. I had heard enough revolutionary talk among my workmen fellow-passengers ; but most of it was hot and turgid, and fell discredited from the lips of unsuccessful men. This man was calm ; he had attained prosperity and ease ; he disapproved the policy which had been pursued by labor in the past; and yet this was his panacea,—to rend the old country from end to end, and from top to bottom, and in clamor and civil discord remodel it with the hand of violence.

The Stowaways

ON the Sunday, among a party of
men who were talking in our
companion, Steerage No. 2 and 3, we
remarked a new figure. He wore tweed
clothes, well enough made if not very
fresh, and a plain smoking-cap. His
face was pale, with pale eyes, and spirit-
edly enough designed; but though not
yet thirty, a sort of blackguardly de-
generation had already overtaken his
features. The fine nose had grown
fleshy towards the point, the pale eyes
were sunk in fat. His hands were strong
and elegant; his experience of life evi-
dently varied; his speech full of pith
and verve; his manners forward, but
perfectly presentable. The lad who
helped in the second cabin told me, in

answer to a question, that he did not
know who he was, but thought, 'by his
way of speaking, and because he was so
polite, that he was some one from the
saloon.'

I was not so sure, for to me there was
something equivocal in his air and bear-
ing. He might have been, I thought,
the son of some good family who had
fallen early into dissipation and run
from home. But, making every allowance, how admirable was his talk! I
wish you could have heard him tell his
own stories. They were so swingingly
set forth, in such dramatic language,
and illustrated here and there by such
luminous bits of acting, that they could
only lose in any reproduction. There
were tales of the P. and O. Company,
where he had been an officer; of the
East Indies, where in former years he
had lived lavishly; of the Royal Engineers, where he had served for a period;

and of a dozen other sides of life, each introducing some vigorous thumb-nail portrait. He had the talk to himself that night, we were all so glad to listen. The best talkers usually address themselves to some particular society; there they are kings, elsewhere camp-followers, as a man may know Russian and yet be ignorant of Spanish; but this fellow had a frank, headlong power of style, and a broad, human choice of subject, that would have turned any circle in the world into a circle of hearers. He was a Homeric talker, plain, strong, and cheerful; and the things and the people of which he spoke became readily and clearly present to the minds of those who heard him. This, with a certain added coloring of rhetoric and rodomontade, must have been the style of Burns, who equally charmed the ears of duchesses and hostlers.

8

Yet freely and personally as he spoke,
many points remained obscure in his
narration. The Engineers, for instance,
was a service which he praised highly;
it is true there would be trouble with
the sergeants; but then the officers were
gentlemen, and his own, in particular,
one among ten thousand. It sounded
so far exactly like an episode in the
rakish, topsy-turvy life of such an one
as I had imagined. But then there
came incidents more doubtful, which
showed an almost impudent greed after
gratuities, and a truly impudent disre-
gard for truth. And then there was the
tale of his departure. He had wearied,
it seems, of Woolwich, and one fine
day, with a companion, slipped up to
London for a spree. I have a suspicion
that spree was meant to be a long one;
but God disposes all things; and one
morning, near Westminster Bridge.
whom should he come across but the

very sergeant who had recruited him at
first! What followed? He himself
indicated cavalierly that he had then resigned. Let us put it so. But these
resignations are sometimes very trying.

At length, after having delighted us
for hours, he took himself away from
the companion; and I could ask Mackay
who and what he was. 'That?' said
Mackay. 'Why, that's one of the stowaways.'

'No man,' said the same authority,
'who has had anything to do with the
sea, would ever think of paying for a
passage.' I give the statement as
Mackay's, without endorsement; yet I
am tempted to believe that it contains a
grain of truth; and if you add that the
man shall be impudent and thievish, or
else dead-broke, it may even pass for a
fair representation of the facts. We
gentlemen of England who live at home
at ease have, I suspect very insufficient

ideas on the subject. All the world over, people are stowing away in coal-holes and dark corners, and when ships are once out to sea, appearing again, begrimed and bashful, upon deck. The career of these sea-tramps partakes largely of the adventurous. Thay may be poisoned by coal-gas, or die by starvation in their place of concealment; or when found they may be clapped at once and ignominiously into irons, thus to be carried to their promised land, the port of destination, and alas! brought back in the same way to that from which they started, and there delivered over to the magistrates and the seclusion of a county jail. Since I crossed the Atlantic, one miserable stowaway was found in a dying state among the fuel, uttered but a word or two, and departed for a farther country than America.

When the stowaway appears on deck,

he has but one thing to pray for ; that
he be set to work, which is the price
and sign of his forgiveness. After half
an hour with a swab or a bucket, he
feels himself as secure as if he had paid
for his passage. It is not altogether a
bad thing for the company, who get
more or less efficient hands for nothing
but a few plates of junk and duff; and
every now and again find themselves
better paid than by a whole family of
cabin passengers. Not long ago, for
instance, a packet was saved from nearly
certain loss by the skill and courage of
a stowaway engineer. As was no more
than just a handsome subscription rewarded him for his success; but even
without such exceptional good fortune,
as things stand in England and America,
the stowaway will often make a good
profit out of his adventure. Four engineers stowed away last summer on the
same ship, the *Circassia;* and before two

days after their arrival each of the four
had found a comfortable berth. This
was the most hopeful tale of emigration
that I heard from first to last ; and as
you see, the luck was for stowaways.

My curiosity was much inflamed by
what I heard ; and the next morning,
as I was making the round of the ship,
I was delighted to find the ex-Royal
Engineer engaged in washing down the
white paint of a deck-house. There
was another fellow at work beside him,
a lad not more than twenty, in the most
miraculous tatters, his handsome face
sown with grains of beauty and lighted
up by expressive eyes. Four stowaways
had been found aboard our ship before
she left the Clyde, but these two had
alone escaped the ignominy of being put
ashore. Alick, my acquaintance of last
night, was Scots by birth, and by trade
a practical engineer ; the other was from
Devonshire, and had been to sea before

the mast. Two people more unlike by
training, character, and habits, it would
be hard to imagine; yet here they were
together, scrubbing paint.

Alick had held all sorts of good situ-
ations, and wasted many opportunities
in life. I have heard him end a story
with these words: ' That was in my golden
days, when I used finger-glasses.' Situation after situation failed him ; then
followed the depression of trade, and
for months he had hung round with
other idlers, playing marbles all day in
the West Park, and going home at
night to tell his landlady how he had
been seeking for a job. I believe this
kind of existence was not unpleasant to
Alick himself, and he might have long
continued to enjoy idleness and a life
on tick ; but he had a comrade, let us
call him Brown, who grew restive. This
fellow was continually threatening to
slip his cable for the States, and at last,

one Wednesday, Glasgow was left wid-
owed of her Brown. Some months
afterwards, Alick met another old chum
in Sauchiehall Street.

'By the by, Alick,' said he, 'I met a
gentleman in New York who was asking
for you.'

'Who was that?' asked Alick.

'The new second engineer on board
the *So-and-so*,' was the reply.

'Well, and who is he?'

'Brown, to be sure.'

For Brown had been one of the fortunate quartette aboard the *Circassia*. If
that was the way of it in the States,
Alick thought it was high time to follow Brown's example. He spent his
last day, as he put it, 'reviewing the
yeomanry,' and the next morning says
he to his landlady, 'Mrs. X., I'll not
take porridge to-day, please; I'll take
some eggs.'

'Why, have you found a job?' she asked, delighted.

'Well, yes,' returned the perfidious Alick ; 'I think I 'll start to-day.'

And so, well lined with eggs, start he did, but for America. I am afraid that landlady has seen the last of him.

It was easy enough to get on board in the confusion that attends a vessel's departure ; and in one of the dark corners of Steerage No. 1, flat in a bunk and with an empty stomach, Alick made the voyage from the Broomielaw to Greenock. That night, the ship's yeoman pulled him out by the heels and had him before the mate. Two other stowaways had already been found and sent ashore ; but by this time darkness had fallen, they were out in the middle of the estuary, and the last steamer had left them till the morning.

'Take him to the forecastle and give

him a meal,' said the mate, 'and see
and pack him off the first thing to-
morrow.'

In the forecastle he had supper, a
good night's rest, and breakfast; and
was sitting placidly with a pipe, fancy-
ing all was over and the game up for
good with that ship, when one of the
sailors grumbled out an oath at him,
with a ' What are you doing there?' and
' Do you call that hiding, anyway?' There
was need of no more; Alick was in
another bunk before the day was older.
Shortly before the passengers arrived,
the ship was cursorily inspected. He
heard the round come down the companion and look into one pen after
another, until they came within two of
the one in which he lay concealed.
Into these last two they did not enter,
but merely glanced from without; and
Alick had no doubt that he was personally favoured in this escape.   It was the

character of the man to attribute nothing to luck and but little to kindness ;
whatever happened to him he had earned
in his own right amply ; favours came
to him from his singular attraction and
adroitness, and misfortunes he had always accepted with his eyes open. Half
an hour after the searchers had departed,
the steerage began to fill with legiti-
mate passengers, and the worst of
Alick's troubles was at an end. He was
soon making himself popular, smoking
other people's tobacco, and politely
sharing their private stock of delicacies,
and when night came he retired to his
bunk beside the others with composure.

Next day by afternoon, Lough Foyle
being already far behind, and only the
rough north-western hills of Ireland
within view, Alick appeared on deck to
court inquiry and decide his fate. As a
matter of fact, he was known to several
on board, and even intimate with one

of the engineers; but it was plainly not the etiquette of such occasions for the authorities to avow their information. Every one professed surprise and anger on his appearance, and he was led prisoner before the captain.

'What have you got to say for yourself?' inquired the captain.

'Not much,' said Alick; 'but when a man has been a long time out of a job, he will do things he would not under other circumstances.'

'Are you willing to work?'

Alick swore he was burning to be useful.

'And what can you do?' asked the captain.

He replied composedly that he was a brass-fitter by trade.

'I think you will be better at engineering?' suggested the officer, with a shrewd look.

'No, sir,' says Alick simply.—'There's

few can beat me at a lie,' was his engaging commentary to me as he recounted the affair.

'Have you been to sea?' again asked the captain.

'I've had a trip on a Clyde steamboat, sir, but no more,' replied the unabashed Alick.

'Well, we must try and find some work for you,' concluded the officer.

And hence we behold Alick, clear of the hot engine-room, lazily scraping paint and now and then taking a pull upon a sheet. 'You leave me alone,' was his deduction. 'When I get talking to a man, I can get round him.'

The other stowaway, whom I will call the Devonian — it was noticeable that neither of them told his name — had both been brought up and seen the world in a much smaller way. His father, a confectioner, died and was closely followed by his mother. His

sisters had taken, I think, to dress-mak-
ing. He himself had returned from
sea about a year ago and gone to live
with his brother, who kept the 'George
Hotel'—'it was not quite a real hotel,'
added the candid fellow—'and had a
hired man to mind the horses.' At first
the Devonian was very welcome; but as
time went on his brother not unnatur-
ally grew cool towards him, and he
began to find himself one too many at
the 'George Hotel.' 'I don't think
brothers care much for you,' he said, as
a general reflection upon life.   Hurt at
this change, nearly penniless, and too
proud to ask for more, he set off on
foot and walked eighty miles to Wey-
mouth, living on the journey as he
could.   He would have enlisted, but he
was too small for the army and too old
for the navy; and thought himself
fortunate at last to find a berth on
board a trading dandy.   Somewhere in

the Bristol Channel, the dandy sprung
a leak and went down; and though the
crew were picked up and brought
ashore by fishermen, they found themselves with nothing but the clothes
upon their back. His next engage-
ment was scarcely better starred; for
the ship proved so leaky, and frightened
them all so heartily during a short passage through the Irish Sea, that the
entire crew deserted and remained
behind upon the quays of Belfast.

Evil days were now coming thick on
the Devonian. He could find no berth
in Belfast, and had to work a passage
to Glasgow on a steamer. She reached
the Broomielaw on a Wednesday: the
Devonian had a bellyful that morning,
laying in breakfast manfully to provide
against the future, and set off along
the quays to seek employment. But he
was now not only penniless, his clothes
had begun to fall in tatters; he had

begun to have the look of a street
Arab; and captains will have nothing
to say to a ragamuffin; for in that
trade, as in all others, it is the coat that
depicts the man. You may hand, reef,
and steer like an angel, but if you have
a hole in your trousers, it is like a mill-
stone round your neck. The Devonian
lost heart at so many refusals. He had
not the impudence to beg; although as
he said, 'when I had money of my
own, I always gave it.' It was only on
Saturday morning, after three whole
days of starvation, that he asked a scone
from a milkwoman, who added of her
own accord a glass of milk. He had
now made up his mind to stow away,
not from any desire to see America, but
merely to obtain the comfort of a place
in the forcastle and a supply of familiar
sea-fare. He lived by begging, always
from milkwomen, and always scones
and milk, and was not once refused. It

was vile wet weather, and he could
never have been dry. By night he
walked the streets, and by day slept
upon Glasgow Green, and heard, in the
intervals of his dozing, the famous
theologians of the spot clear up intricate
points of doctrine and appraise the
merits of the clergy. He had not
much instruction; he could 'read bills
on the street,' but was 'main bad at
writing'; yet these theologians seem to
have impressed him with a genuine
sense of amusement. Why he did not
go to the Sailor's Home I know not; I
presume there is in Glasgow one of
these institutions, which are by far the
happiest and the wisest effort of con-
temporaneous charity; but I must stand
to my author, as they say in old books,
and relate the story as I heard it. In
the meantime, he had tried four times
to stow away in different vessels, and
four times had been discovered and

9

handed back to starvation. The fifth
time was lucky; and you may judge if
he were pleased to be aboard ship again,
at his old work, and with duff twice a
week. He was, said Alick, 'a devil for
the duff.' Or if devil was not the word,
it was one if anything stronger.

The difference in the conduct of the
two was remarkable. The Devonian
was as willing as any paid hand, swarmed
aloft among the first, pulled his natural
weight and firmly upon a rope, and
found work for himself when there was
none to show him. Alick, on the other
hand, was not only a skulker in the grain,
but took a humorous and fine gentle-
manly view of the transaction. He
would speak to me by the hour in osten-
tatious idleness; and only if the bo's'un
or a mate came by, fell-to languidly for
just the necessary time till they were
out of sight. 'I'm not breaking my
heart with it,' he remarked.

Once there was a hatch to be opened near where he was stationed; he watched the preparations for a second or so suspiciously, and then, ' Hullo,' said he, ' here's some real work coming—I'm off,' and he was gone that moment. Again, calculating the six guinea passage-money, and the probable duration of the passage, he remarked pleasantly that he was getting six shillings a day for this job, 'and it's pretty dear to the company at that.' 'They are making nothing by me,' was another of his observations; 'they're making something by that fellow.' And he pointed to the Devonian, who was just then busy to the eyes.

The more you saw of Alick, the more, it must be owned, you learned to despise him. His natural talents were of no use either to himself or others; for his character had degenerated like his face, and become pulpy and pretentious.

Even his power of persuasion, which was certainly very surprising, stood in some danger of being lost or neutralised by over-confidence. He lied in an aggressive, brazen manner, like a pert criminal in the dock; and he was so vain of his own cleverness that he could not refrain from boasting, ten minutes after, of the very trick by which he had deceived you. 'Why, now I have more money than when I came on board,' he said one night, exhibiting a sixpence, 'and yet I stood myself a bottle of beer before I went to bed yesterday. And as for tobacco, I have fifteen sticks of it.' That was fairly successful indeed; yet a man of his superiority, and with a less obtrusive policy, might, who knows? have got the length of half a crown. A man who prides himself upon persuasion should learn the persuasive faculty of silence, above all as to his own misdeeds. It is only in the farce and for

dramatic purposes that Scapin enlarges
on his peculiar talents to the world at
large.

Scapin is perhaps a good name for
this clever, unfortunate Alick; for at the
bottom of all his misconduct there was
a guiding sense of humour that moved
you to forgive him. It was more than
half a jest that he conducted his existence. 'Oh, man,' he said to me once
with unusual emotion, like a man thinking of his mistress, 'I would give up
anything for a lark.'

It was in relation to his fellow-stow-
away that Alick showed the best, or
perhaps I should say, the only, good
points of his nature. 'Mind, you,'
he said suddenly, changing his tone,
'mind you that's a good boy. He
wouldn't tell you a lie. A lot of them
think he is a scamp because his clothes
are ragged, but he isn't; he's as good as
gold.' To hear him, you become aware

that Alick himself had a taste for virtue.
He thought his own idleness and the
other's industry equally becoming.   He
was no more anxious to insure his own
reputation as a liar than to uphold the
truthfulness of his companion; and he
seemed unaware of what was incongruous in his attitude, and was plainly sin-
cere in both characters.

It was not surprising that he should
take an interest in the Devonian, for the
lad worshipped and served him in love
and wonder.   Busy as he was, he would
find time to warn Alick of an approach-
ing officer, or even to tell him that the
coast was clear, and he might slip off
and smoke a pipe in safety.   'Tom,' he
once said to him, for that was the name
which Alick ordered him to use, 'if you
don't like going to the galley, I'll go
for you.   You ain't used to this kind of
thing, you ain't.   But I'm a sailor; and
I can understand the feelings of any

fellow, I can.' Again, he was hard up,
and casting about for some tobacco, for
he was not so liberally used in this respect as others perhaps less worthy,
when Alick offered him the half of one
of his fifteen sticks. I think, for my
part, he might have increased the offer
to a whole one, or perhaps a pair of
them, and not lived to regret his liber-
ality. But the Devonian refused. 'No,'
he said, ' you 're a stowaway like me; I
won't take it from you, I 'll take it from
some one who's not down on his luck.'

It was notable in this generous lad
that he was strongly under the influence
of sex. If a woman passed near where
he was working, his eyes lit up, his
hand paused, and his mind wandered
instantly to other thoughts. It was
natural that he should exercise a fasci-
nation proportionally strong upon
women. He begged, you will remember, from women only, and was never

refused. Without wishing to explain
away the charity of those who helped
him, I cannot but fancy he may have
owed a little to his handsome face, and
to that quick, responsive nature, formed
for love, which speaks eloquently
through all disguises, and can stamp an
impression in ten minutes' talk or an
exchange of glances. He was the more
dangerous in that he was far from bold,
but seemed to woo in spite of himself,
and with a soft and pleading eye.
Ragged as he was, and many a scare-
crow is in that respect more comfortably
furnished, even on board he was not
without some curious admirers.

There was a girl among the passengers, a tall, blonde, handsome, strapping
Irishwoman, with a wild, accommodat-
ing eye, whom Alick had dubbed
Tommy, with that transcendental appro-
priateness that defies analysis. One
day the Devonian was lying for warmth

in the upper stoke-hole, which stands
open on the deck, when Irish Tommy
came past, very neatly attired, as was
her custom.

'Poor fellow,' she said, stopping,
'you haven't a vest.'

'No,' he said; 'I wish I 'ad.'

Then she stood and gazed on him in
silence, until, in his embarrassment, for
he knew not how to look under this
scrutiny, he pulled out his pipe and
began to fill it with tobacco.

'Do you want a match?' she asked.
And before he had time to reply, she
ran off and presently returned with
more than one.

That was the beginning and the
end, as far as our passage is concerned, of what I will make bold to
call this love-affair. There are many
relations which go on to marriage and
last during a lifetime, in which less
human feeling is engaged than in this

scene of five minutes at the stoke-
hole.

Rigidly speaking, this would end the
chapter of the stowaways; but in a
larger sense of the word I have yet more
to add.   Jones had discovered and
pointed out to me a young woman who
was remarkable among her fellows for
a pleasing and interesting air.   She
was poorly clad, to the verge, if not
over the line, of disrespectability, with a
ragged old jacket and a bit of a sealskin
cap no bigger than your fist; but her
eyes, her whole expression, and her manner, even in ordinary moments, told of
a true womanly nature, capable of love,
anger, and devotion.   She had a look,
too, of refinement, like one who might
have been a better lady than most, had
she been allowed the opportunity.
When alone she seemed pre-occupied
and sad; but she was not often alone;
there was usually by her side a heavy,

dull, gross man in rough clothes, chary
of speech and gesture—not from cau-
tion, but poverty of disposition; a man
like a ditcher, unlovely and uninterest-
ing; whom she petted and tended and
waited on with her eyes as if he had
been Amadis of Gaul. It was strange
to see this hulking fellow dog-sick, and
this delicate, sad woman caring for him.
He seemed, from first to last, insensible
of her caresses and attentions, and she
seemed unconscious of his insensibility.
The Irish husband, who sang his wife to
sleep, and this Scottish girl serving her
Orson, were the two bits of human
nature that most appealed to me throughout the voyage.

On the Thursday before we arrived,
the tickets were collected; and soon a
rumour began to go round the vessel; and this girl, with her bit of sealskin cap, became the center of whiper-
ing and pointed fingers. She also, it

was said, was a stowaway of a sort; for she was on board with neither ticket nor money; and the man with whom she travelled was the father of a family, who had left wife and children to be hers. The ship's officers discouraged the story, which may therefore have been a story and no more; but it was believed in the steerage, and the poor girl had to encounter many curious eyes from that day forth.

Personal Experience and Review

TRAVEL is of two kinds; and this voyage of mine across the ocean combined both. 'Out of my country and myself I go,' sings the old poet: and I was not only travelling out of my country in latitude and longitude, but out of myself in diet, associates, and consideration. Part of the interest and a great deal of the amusement flowed, at least to me, from this novel situation in the world.

I found that I had what they call fallen in life with absolute success and verisimilitude. I was taken for a steerage passenger; no one seemed surprised that I should be so; and there was nothing but the brass plate between decks to remind

me that I had once been a gentleman.
In a former book, describing a former
journey, I expressed some wonder that
I could be readily and naturally taken
for a pedlar, and explained the accident
by the difference of language and manners between England and France. I
must now take a humbler view; for here
I was among my own countrymen,
somewhat roughly clad, to be sure, but
with every advantage of speech and
manner; and I am bound to confess
that I passed for nearly anything you
please except an educated gentleman.
The sailors called me 'mate,' the officers
addressed me as 'my man,' my comrades
accepted me without hesitation for a
person of their own character and experience, but with some curious information. One, a mason himself, believed
I was a mason; several, and among
these at least one of the seamen, judged
me to be a petty officer in the American

navy; and I was so often set down for a
practical engineer that at last I had not
the heart to deny it.   From all these
guesses I drew one conclusion, which
told against the insight of my companions.   They might be close observers in
their own way, and read the manners in
the face; but it was plain that they did
not extend their observation to the
hands.

To the saloon passengers also I sustained my part without a hitch.   It is
true I came little in their way; but when
we did encounter, there was no recogni-
tion in their eye, although I confess I
sometimes courted it in silence.   All
these, my inferiors and equals, took me,
like the transformed monarch in the
story, for a mere common, human man.
They gave me a hard, dead look, with
the flesh about the eye kept unrelaxed.

With the women this surprised me
less, as I had already experimented on

the sex by going abroad through a
suburban part of London simply attired
in a sleeve-waistcoat. The result was
curious. I then learned for the first
time, and by the exhaustive process,
how much attention ladies are accus-
tomed to bestow on all male creatures of
their own station; for, in my humble
rig, each one who went by me caused me
a certain shock of surprise and a sense
of something wanting. In my normal
circumstances, it appeared every young
lady must have paid me some tribute of
a glance; and though I had often not
detected it when it was given, I was well
aware of its absence when it was with-
held. My height seemed to decrease
with every woman who passed me, for
she passed me like a dog. This is one
of my grounds for supposing that what
are called the upper classes may sometimes produce a disagreeable impression
in what are called the lower; and I wish

some one would continue my experiment, and find out exactly at what stage of toilette a man becomes invisible to the well-regulated female eye.

Here on shipboard the matter was put to a more complete test; for, even with the addition of speech and manner, I passed among the ladies for precisely the average man of the steerage. It was one afternoon that I saw this demonstrated. A very plainly dressed woman was taken ill on deck. I think I had the luck to be present at every sudden seizure during all the passage; and on this occasion found myself in the place of importance, supporting the sufferer. There was not only a large crowd immediately around us, but a considerable knot of saloon passengers leaning over our heads from the hurricane-deck. One of these, an elderly managing woman, hailed me with counsels. Of course I had to reply; and as the talk

10

went on, I began to discover that the
whole group took me for the husband.
I looked upon my new wife, poor creature, with mingled feelings; and I must
own she had not even the appearance of
the poorest class of city servant-maids,
but looked more like a country wench
who should have been employed at a
roadside inn. Now was the time for me
to go and study the brass plate.

To such of the officers as knew about
me—the doctor, the purser, and the
stewards—I appeared in the light of a
broad joke. The fact that I spent the
better part of my day in writing had
gone abroad over the ship and tickled
them all prodigiously. Whenever they
met me they referred to my absurd
occupation with familiarity and breadth
of humorous intention. Their manner
was well calculated to remind me of my
fallen fortunes. You may be sincerely
amused by the amateur literary efforts

of a gentleman, but you scarce publish the feeling to his face. 'Well!' they would say: 'still writing?' And the smile would widen into a laugh. The purser came one day into the cabin, and, touched to the heart by my misguided industry, offered me some other kind of writing, 'for which,' he added pointedly, 'you will be paid.' This was nothing else than to copy out the list of passengers.

Another trick of mine which told against my reputation was my choice of roosting-place in an active draught upon the cabin floor. I was openly jeered and flouted for this eccentricity ; and a considerable knot would sometimes gather at the door to see my last dispositions for the night. This was embarrassing, but I learned to support the trial with equanimity.

Indeed I may say that, upon the whole, my new position sat lightly and

naturally upon my spirits. I accepted
the consequences with readiness, and
found them far from difficult to bear.
The steerage conquered me; I con-
formed more and more to the type of
the place, not only in manner but at
heart, growing hostile to the officers and
cabin passengers who looked down
upon me, and day by day greedier for
small delicacies. Such was the result,
as I fancy, of a diet of bread and butter,
soup and porridge. We think we have
no sweet tooth as long as we are full to
the brim of molasses; but a man must
have sojourned in the workhouse before
he boasts himself indifferent to dainties.
Every evening, for instance, I was more
and more pre-occupied about our
doubtful fare at tea. If it was delicate
my heart was much lightened; if it was
but broken fish I was proportionally
downcast. The offer of a little jelly
from a fellow-passenger more provident

than myself caused a marked elevation
in my spirits. And I would have gone
to the ship's end and back again for an
oyster or a chipped fruit.

In other ways I was content with my
position. It seemed no disgrace to be
confounded with my company; for I
may as well declare at once I found
their manners as gentle and becoming
as those of any other class. I do not
mean that my friends could have sat
down without embarrassment and laugh-
able disaster at the table of a duke.
That does not imply an inferiority of
breeding, but a difference of usage.
Thus I flatter myself that I conducted
myself well among my fellow-passengers; yet my most ambitious hope is not
to have avoided faults, but to have com-
mitted as few as possible. I know too
well that my tact is not the same as
their tact, and that my habit of a different society constituted, not only no

qualification, but a positive disability to move easily and becomingly in this. When Jones complimented me—because I 'managed to behave very pleasantly' to my fellow-passengers, was how he put it—I could follow the thought in his mind, and knew his compliment to be such as we pay foreigners on their proficiency in English. I dare say this praise was given me immediately on the back of some unpardonable solecism, which had led him to review my conduct as a whole. We are all ready to laugh at the ploughman among lords; we should consider also the case of a lord among the ploughmen. I have seen a lawyer in the house of a Hebridean fisherman; and I know, but nothing will induce me to disclose, which of these two was the better gentleman. Some of our finest behaviour, though it looks well enough from the boxes, may seem even brutal to the gallery. We boast too often manners that are parochial rather than universal ; that, like a country wine, will not bear transportation for a hundred miles, nor from the parlour to the kitchen. To be a gentleman is to be one all the world over, and in every relation and grade of society. It is a high calling, to which a man must first be born, and then devote himself for life. And, unhappily, the manners of a certain so-called upper grade have a kind of currency, and meet with a certain external acceptation throughout all the others, and this tends to keep us well satisfied with slight acquirements and the amateurish accomplishments of a clique. But manners, like art, should be human and central.

Some of my fellow-passengers, as I now moved among them in a relation of equality, seemed to me excellent gentlemen. They were not rough, nor

hasty, nor disputatious; debated pleasantly, differed kindly; were helpful,
gentle, patient, and placid. The type
of manners was plain, and even heavy;
there was little to please the eye, but
nothing to shock; and I thought gen-
tleness lay more nearly at the spring of
behavior than in many more ornate and
delicate societies. I say delicate, where
I cannot say refined; a thing may be
fine, like ironwork, without being delicate like lace. There was here less
delicacy; the skin supported more cal-
lously the natural surface of events, the
mind received more bravely the crude
facts of human existence; but I do not
think that there was less effective refinement, less consideration for others, less
polite suppression of self. I speak of
the best among my fellow-passengers;
for in the steerage, as well as in the saloon, there is a mixture. Those, then,
with whom I found myself in sympathy,

and of whom I may therefore hope to write with a greater measure of truth, were not only as good in their manners, but endowed with very much the same natural capacities, and about as wise in deduction, as the bankers and barristers of what is called society. One and all were too much interested in disconnected facts, and loved information for its own sake with too rash a devotion; but people in all classes display the same appetite as they gorge themselves daily with the miscellaneous gossip of the newspaper. Newspaper reading, as far as I can make out, is often rather a sort of brown study than an act of culture. I have myself palmed off yesterday's issue on a friend, and seen him re-peruse it for a continuance of minutes with an air at once refreshed and solemn. Workmen, perhaps, pay more attention; but though they may be eager listeners, they have rarely seemed to me either willing or careful thinkers. Culture is not measured by the greatness of the field which is covered by our knowledge, but by the nicety with which we can perceive relations in that field, whether great or small. Workmen, certainly those who were on board with me, I found wanting in this quality or habit of the mind. They did not perceive relations, but leaped to a so-called cause, and thought the problem settled. Thus the cause of everything in England was the form of government, and the cure for all evils was, by consequence, a revolution. It is surprising how many of them said this, and that none should have had a definite thought in his head as he said it. Some hated the Church because they disagreed with it; some hated Lord Beaconsfield because of war and taxes; all hated the masters, possibly with reason. But these feelings were not at the root of the matter ; the true reasoning of their souls ran thus — I have not got on ; I ought to have got on; if there was a revolution I should get on. How? They had no idea. Why ? Because — because — well, look at America !

To be politically blind is no distinction ; we are all so, if you come to that. At bottom, as it seems to me, there is but one question in modern home politics, though it appears in many shapes, and that is the question of money ; and but one political remedy, that the people should grow wiser and better. My workmen fellow-passengers were as impatient and dull of hearing on the second of these points as any member of Parliament; but they had some glimmerings of the first. They would not hear of improvement on their part, but wished the world made over again in a crack, so that they might remain improvident and idle and debauched,

and yet enjoy the comfort and respect
that should accompany the opposite
virtues; and it was in this expectation,
as far as I could see, that many of them
were now on their way to America.
But on the point of money they saw
clearly enough that inland politics, so
far as they were concerned, were redu-
cible to the question of annual income ;
a question which should long ago have
been settled by a revolution, they did
not know how, and which they were
now about to settle for themselves, once
more they knew not how, by crossing
the Atlantic in a steamship of considerable tonnage.

And yet it has been amply shown
them that the second or income question is in itself nothing, and may as
well be left undecided, if there be no
wisdom and virtue to profit by the
change.   It is not by a man's purse, but
by his character, that he is rich or poor.

Barney will be poor, Alick will be poor, Mackay will be poor; let them go where they will, and wreck all the governments under heaven, they will be poor until they die.

Nothing is perhaps more notable in the average workman than his surprising idleness, and the candor with which he confesses to the failing. It has to me been always something of a relief to find the poor, as a general rule, so little oppressed with work. I can in consequence enjoy my own more fortunate beginning with a better grace. The other day I was living with a farmer in America, an old frontiersman, who had worked and fought, hunted and farmed, from his childhood up. He excused himself for his defective education on the ground that he had been overworked from first to last. Even now, he said, anxious as he was, he had never the time to take up a book. In conse-

quence of this, I observed him closely ;
he was occupied for four or, at the extreme outside, for five hours out of the
twenty-four, and then principally in
walking ; and the remainder of the day
he passed in horn idleness, either eating
fruit or standing with his back against
a door.   I have known men do hard
literary work all morning, and then un-
dergo quite as much physical fatigue
by way of relief as satisfied this powerful frontiersman for the day.   He, at
least, like all the educated class, did so
much homage to industry as to persuade
himself he was industrious.   But the
average mechanic recognizes his idleness
with effrontery ; he has even, as I am
told, organized it.

I give the story as it was told me, and
it was told me for a fact.   A man fell
from a housetop in the city of Aberdeen,
and was brought into hospital with
broken bones.   He was asked what was

his trade, and replied that he was a
tapper.   No one had ever heard of such
a thing before ; the officials were filled
with curiosity ; they besought an expla-
nation.   It appeared that when a party
of slaters were engaged upon a roof,
they would now and then be taken with
a fancy for the public-house.   Now a
seamstress, for example, might slip away
from her work and no one be the wiser;
but if these fellows adjourned, the tapping of the mallets would cease, and
thus the neighbourhood be advertised
of their defection.   Hence the career of
the tapper.   He has to do the tapping
and keep up an industrious bustle on
the housetop during the absence of the
slaters.   When he taps for only one or
two the thing is child's-play, but when
he has to represent a whole troop, it is
then that he earns his money in the
sweat of his brow.   Then must he bound
from spot to spot, reduplicate, tripli-

cate, sexduplicate his single personality, and swell and hasten his blows, until he produce a perfect illusion for the ear, and you would swear that a crowd of emulous masons were continuing merrily to roof the house. It must be a strange sight from an upper window.

I heard nothing on board of the tapper; but I was astonished at the stories told by my companions. Skulking, shirking, malingering, were all established tactics, it appeared. They could see no dishonesty where a man who is paid for an hour's work gives half an hour's consistent idling in its place. Thus the tapper would refuse to watch for the police during a burglary, and call himself an honest man. It is not sufficiently recognized that our race detests to work. If I thought that I should have to work every day of my life as hard as I am working now, I should be tempted to give up the struggle.   And the workman early begins on his career of toil.   He has never had his fill of holidays in the past, and his prospect of holidays in the future is both distant and uncertain.   In the circumstances, it would require a high degree of virtue not to snatch alleviations for the moment.

There were many good talkers on the ship ; and I believe good talking of a certain sort is a common accomplishment among working men.   Where books are comparatively scarce, a greater amount of information will be given and received by word of mouth ; and this tends to produce good talkers, and, what is no less needful for conversation, good listeners.   They could all tell a story with effect.   I am sometimes tempted to think that the less literary class show always better in narration ; they have so much more patience with detail, are so much less hurried to reach

II

the points, and preserve so much juster a proportion among the facts. At the same time their talk is dry ; they pursue a topic ploddingly, have not an agile fancy, do not throw sudden lights from unexpected quarters, and when the talk is over they often leave the matter where it was. They mark time instead of marching. They think only to argue, not to reach new conclusions, and use their reason rather as a weapon of offence than as a tool for self-improvement. Hence the talk of some of the cleverest was unprofitable in result, because there was no give and take ; they would grant you as little as possible for premise, and begin to dispute under an oath to conquer or to die.

But the talk of a workman is apt to be more interesting than that of a wealthy merchant, because the thoughts, hopes, and fears of which the workman's life is built lie nearer to necessity

and nature. They are more immediate
to human life. An income calculated
by the week is a far more human thing
than one calculated by the year, and a
small income, simply from its smallness,
than a large one. I never wearied list-
ening to the details of a workman's
economy, because every item stood for
some real pleasure. If he could afford
pudding twice a week, you know that
twice a week the man ate with genuine
gusto and was physically happy ; while
if you learn that a rich man has seven
courses a day, ten to one the half of
them remain untasted, and the whole is
but misspent money and a weariness to
the flesh.

The difference between England and
America to a working man was thus
most humanly put to me by a fellow-
passenger: 'In America,' said he, 'you
get pies and puddings.' I do not hear
enough, in economy books, of pies and

pudding. A man lives in and for the
delicacies, adornments, and accidental
attributes of life, such as pudding to eat
and pleasant books and theatres to oc-
cupy his leisure. The bare terms of
existence would be rejected with con-
tempt by all. If a man feeds on bread
and butter, soup and porridge, his appetite grows wolfish after dainties. And
the workman dwells in a borderland,
and is always within sight of those cheer-
less regions where life is more difficult
to sustain than worth sustaining. Every
detail of our existence, where it is worth
while to cross the ocean after pie and
pudding, is made alive and enthralling
by the presence of genuine desire ; but
it is all one to me whether Crœsus has a
hundred or a thousand thousands in the
bank. There is more adventure in the
life of the working man who descends
as a common soldier into the battle of
life, than in that of the millionaire who

sits apart in an office, like Von Moltke,
and only directs the manœuvres by tele-
graph.   Give me to hear about the
career of him who is in the thick of the
business ; to whom one change of market means an empty belly, and another
a copious and savoury meal.   This is
not the philosophical, but the human
side of economics ; it interests like a
story ; and the life of all who are thus
situated partakes in a small way of the
charm of *Robinson Crusoe;* for every
step is critical, and human life is presented to you naked and verging to its
lowest terms.

New York

AS we drew near to New York I was
at first amused, and then somewhat
staggered, by the cautious and the grisly
tales that went the round. You would
have thought we were to land upon a
cannibal island. You must speak to no
one in the streets, as they would not
leave you till you were rooked and
beaten. You must enter a hotel with
military precautions; for the least you
had to apprehend was to awake next
morning without money or baggage, or
necessary raiment, a lone forked radish
in a bed; and if the worst befell, you
would instantly and mysteriously disappear from the ranks of mankind.

I have usually found such stories cor-
respond to the least modicum of fact.

161

Thus I was warned, I remember, against
the roadside inns of the Cevennes, and
that by a learned professor; and when
I reached Pradelles the warning was
explained, it was but the far-away
rumor and reduplication of a single
terrifying story already half a century
old, and half forgotten in the theatre of
the events. So I was tempted to make
light of these reports against America.
But we had on board with us a man
whose evidence it would not do to put
aside. He had come near these perils
in the body; he had visited a robber
inn. The public has an old and well-
grounded favour for this class of inci-
dent, and shall be gratified to the best
of my power.

My fellow-passenger, whom we shall
call M'Naughten, had come from New
York to Boston with a comrade, seeking work. They were a pair of rattling
blades; and, leaving their baggage at

the station, passed the day in beer-sa-
loons, and with congenial spirits, until
midnight struck. Then they applied
themselves to find a lodging, and walked
the streets till two, knocking at houses
of entertainment and being refused
admittance, or themselves declining the
terms. By two the inspiration of their
liquor had begun to wear off; they
were weary and humble, and after a
great circuit found themselves in the
same street where they had begun their
search, and in front of a French hotel
where they had already sought accom-
modation. Seeing the house still open,
they returned to the charge. A man in
a white cap sat in an office by the door.
He seemed to welcome them more
warmly than when they had first presented themselves, and the charge for
the night had somewhat unaccountably
fallen from a dollar to a quarter. They
thought him ill-looking, but paid their

quarter apiece, and were shown upstairs to the top of the house. There, in a small room, the man in the white cap wished them pleasant slumbers.

It was furnished with a bed, a chair, and some conveniences. The door did not lock on the inside; and the only sign of adornment was a couple of framed pictures, one close above the head of the bed, and the other opposite the foot, and both curtained, as we may sometimes see valuable water-colours, or the portraits of the dead, or works of art more than usually skittish in the subject. It was perhaps in the hope of finding something of this last description that M'Naughten's comrade pulled aside the curtain of the first. He was startlingly disappointed. There was no picture. The frame surrounded, and the curtain was designed to hide, an oblong aperture in the partition, through which they looked forth into the dark corridor. A person standing without could easily take a purse from under the pillow, or even strangle a sleeper as he lay abed. M'Naughten and his comrade stared at each other like Vasco's seamen, 'with a wild surmise;' and then the latter, catching up the lamp, ran to the other frame and roughly raised the curtain. There he stood, petrified; and M'Naughten, who had followed, grasped him by the wrist in terror. They could see into another room, larger in size than that which they occupied, where three men sat crouching and silent in the dark. For a second or so these five persons looked each other in the eyes, then the curtain was dropped, and M'Naughten and his friend made but one bolt of it out of the room and down stairs. The man in the white cap said nothing as they passed him; and they were so pleased to be once more in the open night that

they gave up all notion of a bed, and
walked the streets of Boston till the
morning.

No one seemed much cast down by
these stories, but all inquired after the
address of a respectable hotel ; and I,
for my part, put myself under the conduct of Mr. Jones. Before noon of the
second Sunday we sighted the low
shores outside of New York harbour ;
the steerage passengers must remain on
board to pass through Castle Garden
on the following morning; but we of
the second cabin made our escape along
with the lords of the saloon ; and by six
o'clock Jones and I issued into West
Street, sitting on some straw in the bottom of an open baggage-wagon. It
rained miraculously ; and from that
moment till on the following night I
left New York, there was scarce a lull,
and no cessation of the downpour. The
roadways were flooded ; a loud strident

noise of falling water filled the air ; the restaurants smelt heavily of wet people and wet clothing.

It took us but a few minutes, though it cost us a good deal of money, to be rattled along West Street to our destination : 'Reunion House, No. 10 West Street, one minute's walk from Castle Garden ; convenient to Castle Garden, the Steamboat Landings, California Steamers and Liverpool Ships ; Board and Lodging per day 1 dollar, single meals 25 cents, lodging per night 25 cents; private rooms for families ; no charge for storage or baggage ; satisfaction guaranteed to all persons; Michael Mitchell, Proprietor.' Reunion House was, I may go the length of saying, a humble hostelry. You entered through a long bar-room, thence passed into a little dining-room, and thence into a still smaller kitchen. The furniture was of the plainest ; but the bar was hung in the American taste, with encouraging and hospitable mottoes.

Jones was well known; we were received warmly; and two minutes afterwards I had refused a drink from the proprieter, and was going on, in my plain European fashion, to refuse a cigar, when Mr. Mitchell sternly interposed, and explained the situation. He was offering to treat me, it appeared; whenever an American bar-keeper proposes anything, it must be borne in mind that he is offering to treat; and if I did not want a drink, I must at least take the cigar. I took it bashfully, feeling I had begun my American career on the wrong foot. I did not enjoy that cigar; but this may have been from a variety of reasons, even the best cigar often failing to please if you smoke three-quarters of it in a drenching rain.

For many years America was to me a sort of promised land; ' westward the march of empire holds its way'; the race is for the moment to the young; what has been and what is we imperfectly and obscurely know; what is to be yet lies beyond the flight of our imaginations. Greece, Rome and Judæa are gone by for ever, leaving to generations the legacy of their accomplished work; China still endures, an old-inhabited house in the brand-new city of nations; England has already declined, since she has lost the States; and to these States, therefore, yet undeveloped, full of dark possibilities, and grown, like another Eve, from one rib out of the side of their own old land, the minds of young men in England turn naturally at a certain hopeful period of their age. It will be hard for an American to understand the spirit. But let him imagine a young man, who shall have grown up in an old and rigid circle, following bygone fashions and taught to distrust his

own fresh instincts, and who now suddenly hears of a family of cousins, all
about his own age, who keep house
together by themselves and live far
from restraint and tradition; let him
imagine this, and he will have some im-
perfect notion of the sentiment with
which spirited English youths turn to
the thought of the American Republic.
It seems to them as if, out west, the war
of life was still conducted in the open
air, and on free barbaric terms; as if it
had not yet been narrowed into parlours,
nor begun to be conducted, like some
unjust and dreary arbitration, by com-
promise, costume, forms of procedure,
and sad, senseless self-denial. Which
of these two he prefers, a man with any
youth still left in him will decide rightly
for himself.   He would rather be house-
less than denied a pass-key; rather go
without food than partake of a stalled
ox in stiff, respectable society; rather be

shot out of hand than direct his life
according to the dictates of the world.

He knows or thinks nothing of the
Maine Laws, the Puritan sourness, the
fierce, sordid appetite for dollars, or the
dreary existence of country towns. A
few wild story-books which delighted
his childhood form the imaginative
basis of his picture of America. In
course of time, there is added to this a
great crowd of stimulating details —
vast cities that grow up as by enchant-
ment; the birds, that have gone south
in autumn, returning with the spring to
find thousands camped upon their
marshes, and the lamps burning far and
near along populous streets; forests
that disappear like snow; countries
larger than Britain that are cleared and
settled, one man running forth with his
household gods before another, while
the bear and the Indian are yet scarce
aware of their approach; oil that gushes

12

from the earth; gold that is washed or quarried in the brooks or glens of the Sierras; and all that bustle, courage, action, and constant kaleidoscopic change that Walt Whitman has seized and set forth in his vigorous, cheerful, and loquacious verses.

Here I was at last in America, and was soon out upon New York streets, spying for things foreign. The place had to me an air of Liverpool; but such was the rain that not Paradise itself would have looked inviting. We were a party of four, under two umbrellas; Jones and I and two Scots lads, recent immigrants, and not indisposed to welcome a compatriot. They had been six weeks in New York, and neither of them had yet found a single job or earned a single halfpenny. Up to the present they were exactly out of pocket by the amount of the fare.

The lads soon left us. Now I had

sworn by all my gods to have such a
dinner as would rouse the dead; there
was scarce any expense at which I should
have hesitated; the devil was in it but
Jones and I should dine like heathen
emperors. I set to work, asking after a
restaurant; and I chose the wealthiest
and most gastronomical-looking passers-
by to ask from. Yet, although I had
told them I was willing to pay anything
in reason, one and all sent me off to
cheap, fixed-price houses, where I would
not have eaten that night for the cost of
twenty dinners. I do not know if this
were characteristic of New York, or
whether it was only Jones and I who
looked un-dinerly and discouraged
enterprising suggestions. But at length,
by our own sagacity, we found a French
restaurant, where there was a French
waiter, some fair French cooking, some
so-called French wine, and French coffee to conclude the whole. I never

entered into the feelings of Jack on land
so completely as when I tasted that
coffee.

I suppose we had one of the 'private
rooms for families' at Reunion House.
It was very small, furnished with a bed,
a chair, and some clothes-pegs; and it
derived all that was necessary for the
life of the human animal through two
borrowed lights; one looking into the
passage, and the second opening, without sash into another apartment, where
three men fitfully snored, or in intervals
of wakefulness, drearily mumbled to
each other all night long.   It will be
observed that this was almost exactly
the disposition of the room in
M'Naughten's story.   Jones had the
bed; I pitched my camp upon the floor;
he did not sleep until near morning,
and I, for my part, never closed an eye.

At sunrise I heard a cannon fired;
and shortly afterwards the men in the

next room gave over snoring for good, and began to rustle over their toilettes. The sound of their voices as they talked was low and moaning, like that of people watching by the sick. Jones, who had at last begun to doze, tumbled and murmured, and every now and then opened unconscious eyes upon me where I lay. I found myself growing eerier and eerier, for I daresay I was a little fevered by my restless night, and hurried to dress and get downstairs.

You had to pass through the rain, which still fell thick and resonant, to reach a lavatory on the other side of the court. There were three basinstands, and a few crumpled towels and pieces of wet soap, white and slippery like fish; nor should I forget a looking-glass and a pair of questionable combs. Another Scots lad was here, scrubbing his face with a good will. He had been three months in New York and had not

yet found a single job nor earned a
single halfpenny. Up to the present,
he also was exactly out of pocket by the
amount of the fare. I began to grow
sick at heart for my fellow-emigrants.

Of my nightmare wanderings in New
York I spare to tell. I had a thousand
and one things to do; only the day to
do them in, and a journey across the
continent before me in the evening. It
rained with patient fury; every now and
then I had to get under cover for a
while in order, so to speak, to give my
mackintosh a rest; for under this continued drenching it began to grow damp
on the inside. I went to banks, post-
offices, railway-offices, restaurants, publishers, booksellers, money-changers,
and wherever I went a pool would
gather about my feet, and those who
were careful of their floors would look
on with an unfriendly eye. Wherever I
went, too, the same traits struck me:

the people were all surprisingly rude
and surprisingly kind. The money-
changer cross-questioned me like a
French commissary, asking my age, my
business, my average income, and my
destination, beating down my attempts
at evasion, and receiving my answers in
silence; and yet when all was over, he
shook hands with me up to the elbows,
and sent his lad nearly a quarter of a
mile in the rain to get me books at a
reduction. Again, in a very large publishing and bookselling establishment,
a man, who seemed to be the manager,
received me as I had certainly never
before been received in any human shop,
indicated squarely that he put no faith
in my honesty, and refused to look up
the names of books or give me the
slightest help or information, on the
ground, like the steward, that it was
none of his business. I lost my temper
at last, said I was a stranger in America

and not learned in their etiquette; but
I would assure him, if he went to any
bookseller in England, of more handsome usage.   The boast was perhaps
exaggerated; but like many a long shot,
it struck the gold.   The manager passed
at once from one extreme to the other;
I may say that from that moment he
loaded me with kindness; he gave me
all sorts of good advice, wrote me down
addresses, and came bare-headed into
the rain to point me out a restaurant,
where I might lunch, nor even then did
he seem to think that he had done
enough.   These are (it is as well to be
bold in statement) the manners of
America.   It is this same opposition
that has most struck me in people of
almost all classes and from east to west.
By the time a man had about strung me
up to be the death of him by his insulting
behaviour, he himself would be just upon
the point of melting into confidence and

serviceable attentions. Yet I suspect,
although I have met with the like in so
many parts, that this must be the character of some particular state or group
of states; for in America, and this again
in all classes, you will find some of the
softest-mannered gentlemen in the world.

I was so wet when I got back to
Mitchell's toward the evening, that I
had simply to divest myself of my
shoes, socks and trousers, and leave
them behind for the benefit of New
York city. No fire could have dried
them ere I had to start; and to pack
them in their present condition was to
spread ruin among my other posses-
sions. With a heavy heart I said farewell to them as they lay a pulp in the
middle of a pool upon the floor of
Mitchell's kitchen. I wonder if they
are dry by now. Mitchell hired a man
to carry my baggage to the station,
which was hard by, accompanied me

thither himself, and recommended me
to the particular attention of the officials.   No one could have been kinder.
Those who are out of pocket may go
safely to Reunion House, where they
will get decent meals and find an honest
and obliging landlord.   I owed him
this word of thanks, before I enter fairly
on the second and far less agreeable
chapter of my emigrant experience.